Landing the Internship or Full-Time Job During College

Landing the Internship or Full-Time Job During College

Robert R Peterson

iUniverse, Inc.

New York Lincoln Shanghai

Landing the Internship or Full-Time Job During College

iUniverse books may be ordered through booksellers or by contacting:

iUniverse
2021 Pine Lake Road, Suite 100
Lincoln, NE 68512
www.iuniverse.com
1-800-Authors (1-800-288-4677)

ISBN-13: 978-0-595-36681-1 (pbk)
ISBN-13: 978-0-595-81103-8 (ebk)
ISBN-10: 0-595-36681-3 (pbk)
ISBN-10: 0-595-81103-5 (ebk)

Printed in the United States of America

To my brother, Michael, whom I wish I could spend more time with.

Contents

Acknowledgments

A very special thanks to my father, Robert Donald Peterson, to whom the most credit is due as he painstakingly reviewed each word here after. The work would not be what it is without his insights. A special thanks to David M. Samuel who's mentoring encouraged me to "keep pushing."

Finally, credit is due to the real content creators of *Landing the Internship or Full-Time Job During College*—the contributors:
- Anthony Liguori
- Jay Ayres
- Szymon Swistun
- Tyron J. Stading
- David Winkler
- Sandie Cheung
- Rhett Aultman
- Jeremy Gruenefelder
- Benjamin Lewis
- Carl Irvine
- Bella Voldman
- Ronald Woan
- Heather Jackson
- Trisha Patton
- David Barnes

Foreword

Over the past 30 years in my various roles in corporate leadership, I've been honored to provide mentoring and guidance on a one-on-one basis to several hundreds of early and mid-career professionals. I am now privileged to travel extensively delivering keynote addresses and interactive seminars on career mobility, personal branding and 21st century business technology transformation that touch thousands in similar ways. Throughout these many dialogs, a consistent theme emerges: *Young professionals absolutely must assume direct ownership of the career development process and must become personally accountable for the results of that process.*

Unfortunately, most professionals have not recognized this career self-management imperative, nor have they received much in the way of structured guidance in ways they would perceive as relevant and compelling. I have found this to be particularly true for young professionals in scientific and engineering disciplines. These uniquely skilled and motivated individuals have spent years in rigorous technical coursework and research, and thus have developed deep technical competencies that become very strong career assets for them. However, many have received the misplaced guidance that their technical competence will speak for itself, and have consequently spent precious little time developing the planning and promotional skills that will drive career mobility in the global information culture.

This book will be a game-changer for these young professionals. While there is indeed a dearth of career books crowding the shelves at the bookstores and readily available from Amazon or Google searches, most are written by hiring managers and Human Resources professionals who graduated from college and graduate school decades ago. This book is different, because it is written by young bright minds who have recently made the transition from college to bright careers.

Robert Peterson is his own best career mobility case study. An extremely bright and accomplished young software engineer, Robert has leveraged his significant academic accomplishments and his well-developed skills in communication, col-laboration and career visioning to compile an impressive string of work/life experiences from which he draws valuable insights and best practices. The reader will find his guidance to be useful and even inspiring. We would expect nothing less in a well-thought out how-to guide. However, it doesn't stop there.

What really separates this book from the thousands of others on the market is the integration of many case study stories and concrete examples that have emerged from his research with proven winners. To paraphrase an age old maxim, if you want to learn how to climb a mountain, you'd better start hanging out with successful mountain climbers. Through a series of extensive interviews with 10 other technically oriented "star candidates," all either new hires or interns, Robert has captured the career mobility best practices that each of them have so effectively executed to land their dream jobs; not 20 years ago, but right now in the midst of the most exciting and competitive era in modern history.

The case examples are concrete, very usable, and provide a wealth of motivation for young professionals pursuing careers as engineers or scientists. Sections such as "Quick ways to improve your interviewing technique" and "Common mistakes" provide valuable and actionable insights and strategies. The "Bare minimum to do" sections in each chapter are particularly useful in highlighting the core essentials for the reader who may be constrained by a short period of time. The profiles of each of his "star candidates" even include the actual resume that successfully landed them an interview and eventually, the job. This is about as concrete as any how-to guide can get.

There is one more pleasant surprise emerging from this book. While it was written for and is based on the best practices of engineering and technically-focused professionals, I have found that the guidance and the clear, concrete approaches apply to 21st century professionals of many backgrounds. This is very valuable material, and many, many readers will be able to put these ideas into immediate practice and will achieve powerful results.

I met Robert a few years ago when I was asked to address a group of interns from IBM's Extreme Blue, a program where we tap the minds and creative energy of gifted and accomplished engineering students to provide true value to IBM through very strategic projects. We formed a close mentoring relationship, in which the Mentor has learned at least as much from the Mentee as vice-versa. Considering his unique life experiences, his instincts and his considerable talent (all of which come through strongly in the following pages), I'm honored and humbled that he continues to seek my guidance. I guess I shouldn't be surprised, however. A passion for learning and growth is one of the true hallmarks of 21st century winners.

Enjoy the book. And then, move your feet. Go out and land that dream job!

David Samuel
IBM Industry Executive

 *David Samuel is an IBM Executive currently on loan to More-house College. After a very impressive career—spanning 14 lead-ership roles across 5 different industries, including General Manager of IBM's Global Energy and Utilities industry, Chief Information Officer at NSTAR Electric and Gas Corporation, Vice President of Customer Care for the Boston Edison Company, management consultant with AT&T Solutions and A.T. Kearney and 17 years of industry experience in marketing and sales—David is now sharing his perspective on leadership and business transformation with universities, early-career professionals and emerging business leaders around the country. His private seminars and university lectures provide insights into new models of leadership focused on col-laboration and fact-based decision making, which he believes to be the key character-istics of future leaders. He has also authored numerous white papers, articles and research reports covering a range of technology and business issues. David received his undergraduate degree from the State University of New York and is a graduate of the Harvard Business School.*

1

Building Unmatched Credentials

The most essential elements for successfully landing the job are building strong credentials and then marketing them properly. This chapter will focus on gaining experience; marketing yourself is discussed in *Chapter 2: Crafting a Successful Resume*. The quality and breadth of your experience bounds your potential. The more experience you have, the more opportunities you will have to interact with employers. Out of all the advice offered in this book, this is the most important from which everything else builds upon. Solid experience in your field (i.e. part-time employment, research, pet project, etc.), is often why one candidate is chosen over another.

Your credentials are like stamps of approval. The more stamps of quality you have, the more eager employers will be to talk to you. However, these stamps only attract employers, other factors determine if you land the job. That is why your credentials bound your potential. No matter how talented, charismatic, intelligent, and passionate you are, without good credentials you are less likely to have the opportunity of showcasing such qualities to employers.

A dream job will require stellar credentials. Many of the techniques for becoming a star candidate discussed in this book can be mastered in weeks, but gaining experience is an on-going process. The sooner you start, the higher your potential can become. This chapter is written assuming that you still have a year before graduation or a few months before looking for a summer internship. You must be willing to put serious time and effort into gaining the experience that will make you marketable to employers.

If you don't have a lot of time before your job search begins you may want to skip this chapter for now, but it can still be of great benefit. There is no better way to prepare for an interview or improve your resume than by picking up a pet project related to the employer's business.

DIFFERENTIATING YOURSELF

Unfortunately, most college students think that they will be evaluated for a job the same way they were evaluated for college—by GPA and extracurricular activities. These certainly play a part in your initial evaluation, but in the end, as long as you don't have failing grades, what lands the job is showing employers that you will be an employee that will bring value to their organization which can involve credentials that are quite different. As shocking as it may sound, grades are not the most important factor for employers. If they were, resumes and interviews would not be needed.

Employers often group candidates into GPA ranges. For example, a selective employer may set 3.0/4.0 as a minimum for the first interview unless someone inside the organization makes a recommendation. A candidate with a 3.0 GPA and some experience is on the same playing field as a 4.0 candidate who hasn't built other credentials.

In the end, hiring managers are looking for someone they think will be able to do the job. Employers are often weary of candidates that have an amazing GPA, but no research, project, or professional experience because they suspect such a candidate may lack the maturity, communication skills, and passion for their work environment.

So what qualities matter to employers? Everything employers look for can be mapped to the following principles.

Passion

If you are passionate about your field it is likely that everything else will fall into place. A sign of passion is involvement with professional communities within your field. For example, attending an Aviation Expo if you are an Aerospace Engineer or LinuxWorld if you are a computer scientist. Those could both lead to engaging discussions with employers.

Keep up with trends in your field. A passionate candidate has opinions about his or her field and looks forward to defending them. The Internet is an amazing resource for exploring trends in your field—one that you need to take advantage of in order to be competitive in many respects (see *Chapter 4: Researching an organization*).

You may be thinking to yourself that you can't find anything exciting about the field you are studying. Student coursework can often be dry and monotonous. If you look outside the walls of your classes, it may be surprising what you can get involved in. Keeping up with an industry can be a lot more fun than it was a decade ago—especially in a technical field. For example, you may want to visit blogs (online journals) of famous researchers in your field or contribute to online forums weekly. *Be passionate.*

Industry Perspective

A hiring manager is looking for someone who understands the needs and challenges of their business. If a candidate can gain experience that matches what is done in industry, he or she stands out from the pack. With an industry perspective, you can showcase industry related situations while other candidates are invariably forced to rely on personal experience or coursework to answer questions.

For example, take Rick who is taking a class in circuit board design as an electrical engineer, but everything in the course is done on paper. Thinking outside of the world of academia, Rick decides to learn a popular circuit board design package. He runs through his assignments a second time with the software package and checks his answers. By the end of the class he gives a talk to students and faculty about how the package is one of the most popular tools in industry, some of its key features, and how easy it is to acquire with a student license. Imagine what an employer would say who is recruiting at his university and uses that very same tool.

If you wanted to teach a loved one how to drive a car, would you have them study the schematics of its engine? Would you have them study the history of the construction of automobiles? Perhaps you would have them read some safety regulations, but at some point to learn to drive, you have to get behind the wheel and turn the key. Be the candidate that has turned the key and is driving within your profession. *Build an industry perspective.*

Results-oriented

Hiring managers look for applicants who can get the job done. Period. If your credentials prove that you can solve problems that don't have clear solutions, you can look forward to an exciting career.

You may think "Isn't this essentially the same as having passion?" It is possible for someone to be passionate, but not results-oriented. Have you ever met someone who gets excited about ideas that aren't very practical? There are a lot of highly qualified candidates out there that are better suited to be researchers or free-thinkers. For example, someone who is passionate but is not results-oriented may want to design a television that is voice-controlled when the company mass produces economy TVs.

Employers often seek someone who gets things done and fixes problems, not someone who creates new ones. If you have experience that shows that you have solved a real world problem in a practical way it will make you stand out compared to your peers. *Be results-oriented.*

To summarize, imagine that a house which has been in the family for years needs to be sold and you are interviewing real estate agents. Of all the agents you speak with, you will most likely hire the agent that can demonstrate passion for selling real estate, shows real experience in selling the type of home you own, and has a proven track record of excellent results. The same is true for your profession. You can differentiate yourself from the competition by demonstrating passion, a realistic experience-based perspective of your field, and by proving you can solve problems with a results-oriented approach.

STRATEGIES FOR BUILDING EXPERIENCE

Students often know very well that it is important to differentiate themselves from the competition, but are unsure of how to best build experience in their field. A typical student thinks of an internship or co-op when it comes to gaining experience in college. Without a doubt, there is no stronger credential than actual industry experience on your resume. Pursue internship experience, even if it only loosely relates to your field, as early as possible. However, landing an internship requires credentials and experience just like landing a job. All the rules for landing a full-time position apply to an internship, except that there are far less internship positions available. In other words, it is even more competitive to get a top internship position.

There are many other forms of experience, which require little more than free time that put candidates in a great position when competing for an internship or entry-level position. The rising stars profiled throughout this book, used a stepping stone approach—constantly building stronger credentials by using their previous experience as a prerequisite.

Taking Advantage of Pet Projects

Pet projects can be a great source of credentials. Think of the skills learned in your coursework as a toolkit for building something. You can work on something at your own pace in any way you like. Even if the project doesn't work out as expected or you lose interest, the simple fact that you worked on something outside of your coursework can prove to be impressive.

Example based on a true story

Take the story of Mark who is an industrial engineer. He has just finished his sophomore year, which included a process modeling class where he learned how to model the efficiency of a retail or restaurant business. He decides to try some of the theory he learned in his free time. His aunt owns a pizza business and he volunteers to model how efficient her pizza business is at helping its customers.

His aunt is enthusiastic about the idea and provides him with the details of the floor plan, the schedule of her staff, some numbers regarding how many customers are helped, etc. Mark follows the techniques he learned in his course and finds some inefficiency in the way the business deals with customers. His aunt even takes up some of his suggestions and notices a gain in revenue of four percent per week.

Encouraged by the success of his project, Mark decides to do it on a larger scale by modeling a famous retail store. He contacts the store manager, explains how his analysis helped another business, and volunteers to implement a similar model. The manager is convinced after one of Mark's professors is brought on board as an advisor for the project. Mark is even granted a small amount of money to buy a sophisticated modeling software package. Mark takes several months to learn the software and to model the retail store, but is successful in the end and has some interesting findings. Unfortunately, the store manager has changed by this time and no one returns his calls. He never gets a chance to deliver his analysis.

Even though Mark was not able to see his project through to the end, he has managed to gain some very impressive experience. He's worked with two real businesses and found ways to improve their bottom line. Mark has worked with two modern industrial engineering software packages, and done all of this out of an interest for his field. Mark would have little trouble finding an interview for a prestigious internship.

The Power of Publishing Your Ideas

Publications of any kind can be great ways to build experience. The information age has brought a new wave of techniques to publish ideas and opinions. You may think that publishing is only for graduate students and researchers or students who have a really good relationship with a professor. Don't limit yourself in these ways. Being a rocket scientist is not a requirement. Some of the most fascinating publications are written by people who have an interesting opinion or ask, "what if we did things this way."

You also don't have to publish something you write in a prestigious academic journal for employers to be impressed. If you write something that is published on an industry web site, for example, it may be even more relevant to an employer.

Example

Suppose Julie is a mechanical engineer. She is taking a design class that uses an expensive software product. Fortunately, her university has an academic license for the software program and she can use it for free from her apartment. However, when Julie tries to install the program on her Apple computer at home, it doesn't work. The web site that documents the academic version of the program says it can work on an Apple machine, but it doesn't explain how. She talks to her professor and other students, but everyone else is using a PC. After consulting various forums online and making some calls to the company that makes the software, Julie is finally able to get it to work.

Julie decides to take the notes she's collected along the way and make a quick tutorial for getting the software to work on an Apple machine. After several students ask her for the directions, she volunteers to post the tutorial on her department's web site.

Realizing how many students around the country may benefit from the tutorial as well, she calls the development company that makes the software and volunteers to provide the tutorial in whatever form is most convenient so they can add it to the documentation on their web site. The company is delighted to get her help and admits that they were getting a high call volume on the subject. She politely asks for a guesstimate of how many calls and they report that the issue involved ten percent of their calls.

Julie has just gained great experience in a short period of time. She has contributed to the website of a company that is an industry leader in mechanical design software, and she helped them reduce their call center costs by a quantifiable amount.

A Strong Credential Relevant to Programmers

The following form of experience is becoming just as valuable as traditional industry experience and can improve your potential in a very short period of time; however, it is a stronger fit for a field that involves programming. Open source development is becoming a world-renowned credential. Open source software is licensed such that anyone can use it, even as part of a commercial product, and is built by volunteers from around the world. There are open source projects popping up for anything from operating systems to video games and there is no interview required to get involved. In most cases, getting involved just means going to http://www.sourceforge.net, finding a project that interests you, and downloading the source code.

Nearly every open source project has a bug tracking system that publishes problems that need to be fixed online. The easiest way to get involved is to fix a few bugs. Even if you just fix bugs here and there in your free time, employers will be very impressed with your experience as an open source developer that has worked on a large-scale project mirroring the development of commercial software.

Example

Imagine that Rhonda is a data information science (DIS) student and reads a news article about the epidemic of computer virus attacks on e-mail programs. She looks into alternatives to the most popular e-mail clients and finds an open source equivalent which provides an innovative way to scan and protect against malicious e-mails. After using it for a few days, she realizes that it doesn't have all the functionality she is used to. Since it's an open source project and she is familiar with the programming language it's written in, she decides to contribute to the project by doing bug fixes so the missing features are developed faster. After her first bug fix, she has surpassed the average DIS candidate.

Other Forms of Experience

Hopefully, you have gained some insight into how top candidates guarantee themselves opportunities. They focus on what they can do at the moment to build their credentials with a stepping stone approach, not just on the end goal. Everyone wants a high paying, exciting job, but instead of just searching, smart candidates get involved using whatever skills they have now. Gaining experience should be an ongoing process. The earlier you start the greater your potential will become. Here are some other activities that can help you build unmatched credentials:

- *Participating in competitions sponsored by researchers or employers in your field.* An example would be a competition for a paper or a project. Just the fact that you have participated can be put on your resume later.

- *A part time job or a volunteer position that is related to your field.* Smart students kill two birds with one stone—they build credentials and pay the bills at the same time. Even if you are volunteering, your hard work will ensure your success in the future.

- *Assisting university research in some form.* Research can be a solid form of experience. Additionally, working with professors and grad students may provide you with advice and key connections to industry jobs later. Depending on the employer, research experience can be just as important as industry experience. However, don't expect every employer to be impressed. Some see it as just an extension of your coursework and will pick a candidate with an internship over someone with equivalent research experience.

- *Professional organizations and student clubs.* This is probably the first thing that comes to mind for most students. Being a part of a professional or student organization can show that you are a strong communicator, leader, and organizer. Keep in mind that this sort of experience is very common among college students and it may not differentiate you as well as other activities.

CHOOSING A TOPIC OF INTEREST IN YOUR FIELD

Students are often afraid to pick something to specialize in. You may be worried that if you specialize in something, it will reduce your opportunities. Perhaps you are not sure what to focus on. Don't fall into this trap—find something to be knowledgeable about. Every young professional profiled in this book found something in college to specialize in. Not all of them ended up starting a career in their topic of interest, but it is clear that their expertise in a specific area contributed to their success.

Hiring managers are not impressed by someone who says they are willing to work on anything. Remember, they are looking for someone that will bring value to their organization. A generalist will have his or her resume put in the stack to be looked at later while an aspiring web designer will get forwarded to their Internet technology team. This generalist attitude may portray a candidate as lacking passion.

Imagine that you are an owner of a restaurant that is already well staffed, but your budget does have room to allow for another employee. A young man named John contacts you asking for a position. When you ask him about his experience in the restaurant business, John says he doesn't have any real experience, but is willing to start in any job including cleaning tables, waiting tables, cooking, or delivery driving. Lillian is interested in working for you as well and says she would like to be a waitress. She says it's something she has always wanted to do and she even has a little waitressing experience volunteering at fundraising dinners. Which would you hire? Even though neither candidate is more qualified for the a position, Lillian's application is more appealing because she has defined her desire and interest for waitressing.

What if an employer isn't looking for your specialty? You will be at no disadvantage if you have researched the company properly and know what they are hiring for. Researching a company will be covered in *Chapter 4: Researching an Organization*. It is important to keep in mind that by gaining mastery in a specific area of your field, you are in a small minority compared to your peers. The majority of students complete their coursework without focusing on a specialty and seldom prepare themselves sufficiently before applying for employment. In the case where an employer is not interested in your specialty, you are in the same position as most of your peers. With proper research and the self-marketing strategies covered in this book, you will be able to compete for every position that a generalist can hope for, along with positions tailored for your specialty.

Even if there are no open positions for your specialty, it can lead to opportunities. When employers see real passion they move mountains to add a candidate to their organization. For example, a chemist specializing in processing plastic is offered a position for a large chemical firm; however, it is a customer service position. Within weeks on the job, the young chemist builds a network with other employees of the firm that work in her field of specialty. After a few more months, a transfer is arranged to a new position that is more prestigious than the college entry-level positions she originally sought.

Be creative in deciding what your specialty should be. Students often rely on a professor or choose the most popular area in their field to focus on. It is important to pick something that is relevant to employers. Remember, you want to build an industry perspective; however, jumping on the band-wagon will do little good in differentiating yourself from your peers. The best candidates find something that is both relevant and interesting to them. Remember that passion is a key trait of a star candidate. If you are passionate about your specialty, it will help to differentiate you.

You may want to consider some of the following resources for finding an area to focus on. Specific examples of where to find the Internet sources listed are in "Leveraging the Internet" of *Chapter 4: Researching an Organization.*

- *College interns who have worked for an employer in your field.* Companies often have university representatives who can give you their perspective of what is interesting in industry. Talk to them—find out what they worked on. They will be delighted to tell you about their experiences.

- *Industry news sites.* Just reading a few online publications may be able to give you ideas.

- *Company web sites.* Company web sites often have interesting articles and descriptions of the core areas of their business.

- *Professional Communities.* Join a forum, newsgroup, or e-mail list for an organization of professionals in your field. Asking something as simple as "What would you recommend that I focus on as a business major?" on an e-mail list may bring all sorts of ideas.

Experiment! Try stuff out—you're in college, it's your chance to find something fun. Even if you lose interest, your efforts can be put on your resume as something you have become interested in outside of class. In addition, you can certainly change your specialty if your passion leads to other areas. For example, the author of this book became intensely interested in robotics and computer vision, but later switched his interests to Internet-based distributed systems—completely different engineering disciplines.

COMMON MISTAKES

A mistake that is often made by students is to get involved in something outside of class which can be marketable experience later on, but takes up too much of their valuable time. It is critical that you do a cost benefit analysis of every activity that you participate in.

Example based on a true story

Jeff is a journalism major. He volunteers as a tutor in college algebra at his university. After over a year of volunteering, his university offers him a paid position to spend three hours a day tutoring. Jeff has a scholarship, so he doesn't need the added income very badly, but decides that it is good experience that will give him some extra spending money.

Jeff has fallen into a common trap for many bright students. Jeff understands that he needs to get involved outside of class because it will improve his potential; however, because of his leadership skills and work ethic he naturally becomes more involved in tutoring because he is the best tutor they have. The added value for his time becomes less and less.

Smart candidates jump from activity to activity building on top of each one along the way. There is nothing wrong with Jeff's tutoring experience, but he could have moved on after a semester and gained the same benefit of "Tutor" on his resume.

Stop and think about how much value the activities you are involved with now can really be of use in the future. For instance, focusing all of your free time on being treasurer of the engineering honors club may not be the best use of your valuable time. In the end, it will be one line on your resume—you'll have no advantage over the students who just show up to some of the meetings. You may be a great treasurer and may even be worried how the club could get by without you, but don't do yourself the injustice. You should be worried about how the open source or research project could get by without you.

Some of the brightest students of our time have the wrong perspective of how to be successful in college. They take as many college credits as they can possibly handle and spend every waking moment trying to study so they can raise their GPA by a tenth of a point. When the time comes to apply for a position, they are baffled. They have worked so hard to graduate a year early, have a competitive GPA, and employers don't seem interested at all. From the employer's perspective they are younger, less experienced, and aren't really passionate about their field compared to the competition because they have done little outside of their coursework.

- *Learn to constantly do a cost-benefit analysis of your activities outside of class.*

- *Be weary of credentials that will be on ninety percent of resumes companies see.*

- *Understand the concept of diminishing returns.* If a single credential is taking up a substantial amount of time and the added reward is not clear, consider investing your time in a new activity.

Profile
Anthony Liguori

Who do you work for, what is your official internship title, and where is it located?

I'm a computer science intern for the IBM Extreme Blue program. The project is sponsored by the Linux Technology Center at IBM's Austin, Texas campus.

Was it your first choice?

Yes. This is a dream position for me because it involves two things that I truly believe in—Linux and open source software. I would do it for free. I did have a choice to make, however. I worked for Lockheed Martin part-time for two years. They were very accommodating in offering a position I would be interested in. Raytheon also offered me an internship.

What are some positive aspects of the internship?

For me, the most enjoyable part is that I get to be surrounded by open source technology. Another very attractive aspect is the branding that comes with working on a cutting edge project at IBM. It's a company that is well known as one of the founding forcing during the information age and to be a part of that force will certainly open doors for me in the future.

Extreme Blue really is an internship in a class above the rest in computer science. I'm working on an emerging business opportunity. I'm also on a team of three technical interns and one MBA intern that are all rising stars from around the country. We have the resources and freedom to forge ahead in whatever form we feel is right. It's very much like a start up company environment.

Austin, Texas is also a place that is very new to me. I've always worked and gone to school in New Jersey. I think this experience has shown me how welcoming change can be pivotal in building a career.

What are some negative aspects?

Moving has been a little challenging for me. I've lived up north all my life and I was a little scared to change that. It turns out that Austin is one of top high tech centers of the US and has a really great live music scene. It's not what I had pictured at first. I still feel a little transplanted—it seems that the best things for your career can sometimes be the hardest.

Additionally, it can be hard to get along when everyone you work with is used to being king technically. Everyone here is a strong leader and is used to having an unchallenged opinion within their field. On the other hand, it does result in a lot of fascinating conversation.

What is your typical day like?

I wake up at 7 AM and get to work, which is across the street, at about 8 AM. My typical Extreme Blue day involves a lot of meetings. I usually barely have time to get myself oriented before I have a conference call with experts from an open source project or pitch my project to a touring IBM vice president.

The lab usually gets together to do something for lunch varying between 11 AM and 2 PM. After lunch, I spend my time in meetings or communicating with experts, customers, or peers in one form or another. The lab routinely gets together to do something for dinner around 6 PM. The conversation is almost always an exchange of status between different project teams.

After dinner, I go back to the lab and I'm finally able to do some coding! From 7 PM to 1 AM, I architect, write, and debug C code. My time consists of:

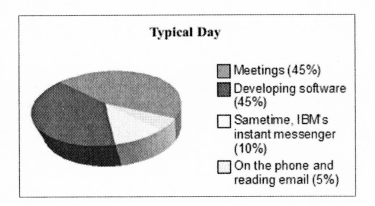

After the day is done I go to bed and repeat—7 days a week. We only have twelve weeks to produce a working prototype and business model. At the end I'll be presenting to the top brass of the company including the CEO at the IBM headquarters in New York. So, I spend every waking moment pushing it forward.

How did you make initial contact with IBM Extreme Blue?

I actually didn't follow the usual application process. I was browsing the web in late April looking for something interesting to do which could compare to a summer position at Lockheed. I came across the Extreme Blue website and noticed the deadline was past to submit an application. I decided to email them and ask if I could still apply. They responded favorably and requested my resume which I submitted in a reply email. They were still filling two more positions, one of which required open source experience.

What was your interview like?

Again, the way I was interviewed is different from the rest of the applicants. At 6 PM, I received a call inviting me to do a phone interview 10 AM the next day. I took every word that was said to me about the position and researched everything humanly possible about it. I read about the IBM Linux mission statement, articles, white papers, emerging product offerings—anything I could get my hands on.

The interview lasted two hours and was roughly 60% behavioral, 20% technical, and 20% HR related.

Have any memorable questions?

Actually the most memorable question was when they asked me whether I'll be graduating in December or May. They were astonished to find out that I just finished my freshman year and that I'm only 19. I now hold the record as the youngest EB intern.

They also asked, "Can you describe a situation where you didn't succeed?" Admitting that you're not infallible is always difficult. I think it's an important question, because it tests humility. My answer came from my work at Lockheed. I was the project lead for an application which I spent an enormous amount of time and energy on. A special group which surveyed the management of technology funding, found a commercial tool that did the exact same task as my team's application.

The funding for our application got cut—I was crushed. I learned a great deal from the ordeal though. It opened my eyes to the real world of software development. No matter how solid your code base is or how talented you are as a software engineer, there are other factors that must be aligned for your work to succeed in the business world. Regardless, at the time, I was not happy about the situation. It was nothing short of a failure to me.

What credentials do you think insured your success?

I've founded five open source projects and contributed to ten. Mastery in the skills they needed, Linux development and C programming, definitely helped. Technical presentations to the Navy showed that I'm a good communicator, not just a code monkey.

Later, I found out that they were having difficulty finding a good candidate looking through what they described as the typical college resume. They all looked the same and had the same basic programming skills learned in class such as Visual Studio or entry-level Java. My accomplishments were a little different and that help enormously.

What advice would you give to someone trying to gain experience in college?

There is no end to the opportunity in your field. All that it requires is a little bit of humility to start in the trenches. Get experience in something you are interested in. It is critical that you get exposed to articles, books, or projects in your field so you know what the work is like in the real world.

The most important advice I can give is to be passionate. The Extreme Blue staff even told me that they often hire someone because they have a twinkle in their eye even when they lack technical ability. I always want someone on my team that embraces a challenge and will work as hard as he or she can by definition—not by necessity.

Note: A the time of this book's publication, Anthony completed his Extreme Blue internship and continued part-time work at IBM on their most strategic Linux projects.

Anthony Liguori

3625 Duval Road 1435   o   Austin, TX 78759   o   (512) 490-6670   o   anthony@codemonkey.ws
http://rockhopper.homelinux.org/resume/

Summary

Strong background in C/C++ development and Unix Systems programming. Contributed to many Open Source projects and have been employed as a software developer for over four years working part-time during school. This resume is available online with hyperlinking to examples of my work for all listed skills.

Education

GPA: 3.64

2002 to Present   **The University of Texas at Austin**
B.S Computer Science with Turing Scholar Honors

2001 to 2002   **Rutgers University**
B.S Computer Science; transferred after freshman year

Experience

2002 to Present   **IBM Corporation**

Interoperability Engineer, Linux Technology Center
- Worked on international team to resolve CRITSITs - problems that occur in multi-million dollar customer accounts that are deemed highest priority. Provided fixes to Samba to increase scalability on the IBM z-Series (mainframe) and tools to analyze network traffic from production environments to generate testing workloads.
- One of four Samba developers within IBM responsible for interacting with the community, advising in pre-sales, resolving escalated support requests, and working on new features in Samba.
- Mentored IBM Extreme Blue project teams including reviewing almost every project team's code for quality.
- Recieved various IBM Invention awards including 5 patent disclosures.

Extreme Blue, Sony/Toshiba/IBM (STI) Design Center
- Helped pilot full-year Extreme Blue program; recruited at various campuses for future Extreme Blue candidates; spoke to student groups about innovation and Linux at IBM
- Analyzed the programmability of the Cell processor--a joint IBM/Sony/Toshiba venture to develop a tera-flop processor--to determine the potential markets for the technology
- Demonstrated proof-of-concept to a large group of IBM Executives and Sony President Mr. Kunitake Ando

Extreme Blue, Linux Technology Center
- First individual to decode new Microsoft protocol--MS-CLDAP. That information is now used in product implementations by IBM, NetApp, EMC and various other NAS vendors
- Built a proof-of-concept demonstration of Linux and Active Directory interoperability using various Open Source packages; enhanced OpenLDAP, MIT Kerberos, and Samba; analyzed and implemented a server for MS-CLDAP
- Presented proof-of-concept to IBM Executives including CEO Sam Palminsano
- Presented work to the SNIA CIFS 2002 conference; asked to participate in drill-down panel discussion

2000 to 2002   **Lockheed Martin Corporation, NE&SS**

ROADSTER Chief Software Architect
- Acted as lead architect and engineer on a FD/FIR system for use on the U.S. Navy's AEGIS Weapons System that controls Arleigh Burke class U.S. Navy Destroyers commissioned after the USS McCampbell (DDG-85)
- Created and maintained high-granularity performance analysis tools for AEGIS; Certified tools to be used in US Navy tactical environments; Chosen for use by Navy over commercial tools such as SOS/9000 Software Developer

Maintaince Engineer
- Resolved bug within the AEGIS Weapons System that were marked as requiring significant system-wide rearchitecting; Several bugs were marked as highest priority by the US Navy

2000 to 2002   **WowIS, Incorporated**
- Developed authentication system for cellular administrator system for use in ComVerse's Latvian cellular network
- Worked as a full-time consultant and lead network administrator managing network services for 40+ employees
- Extended JournyX time card system to produce PDF time reports eliminating a $320k contract-dispute over the legibility of the hand-written time card system

Skills

C, C++, Java, Bash, Csh, Perl, Python, Lisp, ia32 assembly, XHTML, CSS, XML, XSL, Gtk, RedHat Linux, Suse Linux, Gentoo, Windows, Win32, MSRPC, LDAP, Ethereal, Kerberos

2

Crafting a Successful Resume

A resume is a formal advertisement where you are the product that is being marketed. No matter how great your credentials and qualifications are, if employers can't get the key information that differentiates you quickly and easily from your resume, your talents will not be given the opportunities they deserve. Spending the time to make sure you have a well-written resume is the single most effective way to increase opportunities with employers.

Imagine that you are looking through a phone book for a plumber because your kitchen faucet is broken. While browsing the plumbing section you see two large ads. The first is clear and concise with the name, address, phone, and type of work the plumber does. The second looks less professional, is jam-packed with information, is hard to read, and has a typo. Which plumber would you call? The plumber from the second ad may be more competitive, experienced, and honest, but the ad does not reflect this. Don't make the mistake of ineffectively representing yourself with a resume that is thrown together in haste.

This chapter will provide a guide to writing a resume efficiently and effectively. An example candidate, Melissa Barnes, will be used every step of the way to illustrate the process. Preparation is vital; following this guide will give you an edge over the candidate who opens up a word processor and starts typing the night before a career fair.

HOW TO MARKET YOURSELF PROPERLY

The purpose of a resume is to get you a phone call from an employer and to get your foot in the door with the company. This section will help you effectively market yourself with a formal advertisement that stands out from the competition.

The most important thing to keep in mind when writing a resume is that it will not be read like an article or a report. A resume is read on average for fifteen seconds by recruiters. It is scanned briefly and then a decision is made. The only case where a resume is actually read thoroughly is before an interview by the interviewer (and even then, only sometimes). By that point your resume has done its job; the employer already made the call. Thus, if you learn anything from this chapter, learn to write your resume under the assumption that it will be glanced at for fifteen seconds.

When you pick out a can of soup at the grocery store, do the labels make it easy? Do you even have to pickup the jar and read the details before you have made your decision? Your resume needs to be the same way; make it easy for employers to pick out your resume from the rest. Constantly keep in mind that a resume is read by people and people make decisions based on convenience and first impressions. Bold and add white space around points that will catch the reader's eye and put the details in regular print. Oversimplify, evangelize—once you have their attention you can clarify.

Always keep the perspective of a recruiter in mind when you are writing a resume. This is an individual who sees thousands of resumes a year and often looks through stacks of them with different formats. Don't write the resume that frustrates them; write the one that is clear, well formatted, and gets them the information they need quickly.

A recruiter is not an expert in your field and they have not been through your degree program. What may seem like an obvious or routine accomplishment to you may be impressive to them. This can be very helpful when thinking of ways to market your credentials. Have you ever shown your coursework to someone outside of your field? If so, you probably were showered with compliments regarding your superior intellect and talent for a mere weekly homework assignment. What if you showed the same assignment to someone in your class? You would be more likely to be teased for skipping a step in a math equation. Keep this analogy in mind when you are writing a resume.

When developing your resume, be sure it can be read effectively in fifteen seconds. Also, ensure your most marketable credentials are highlighted first and always keep your audience in mind.

START WITH A CONTENT BRAINSTORM

The best way to begin working on a resume is to jot down ideas on paper. Don't think about formality, grammar, or any other rules. Anything goes no matter how silly. Be creative, you are just brainstorming!

Don't limit yourself to accomplishments—think about effective ways to showcase that you are a competent candidate. For example, a positive quote about you from a professor or supervisor could serve as a powerful heading. If you are knowledgeable or interested in a certain area of your field, but don't have official work experience "Enthusiast" or "Evangelist" can be effective. For example, "Auto Cad Enthusiast" may be appropriate if you are a civil engineer and have dabbled with popular industry design tools in various projects.

Here are some more ideas for brainstorming content that can help spark your imagination:

- *Think about every class you have taken.* Coursework can prove to be very impressive especially if not listed as homework or assignments. If a recruiter happens to ask how you got involved in a specific project then certainly explain that it was part of your coursework.

- *Think about any part-time jobs you have taken.* How have you added value to that organization? Have you helped them reduce their operations costs or increase their revenue?

- *Think about anything related to your field outside of coursework.* This includes pet projects, industry events, and interests.

Once your brainstorm for content is finished, group your ideas into categories. There are no set rules for what categories to use. It is often the case that a single credential is its own category. If you have a part time job related to your field and it is your only professional work experience so far, it can be its own category. For example, "Award-winning test engineer."

The two basic types of resumes are functional and chronological. A functional resume concentrates on skills and qualifications. A chronological resume is essentially a timeline showcasing your experience and credentials over time. Which format you adopt may affect your consideration for categorizing the content you have brainstormed. Since you are in college, you may wish to consider combining the strengths of both. For instance, build functional categorizes and list any items within those categories chronologically. For example, a projects section with your project experience listed chronologically.

Here are the most common categories for college resumes to help you generate and group brainstorming ideas:

- *Education.* This is a requirement for a college resume. The university, degree, graduation date, and grade point average should always be listed in some form. It may also include alternate forms of education such as training, certifications, and seminars. High school information is generally not recommended.

- *Objective.* A statement describing what you want to work on and what kind of position you are after.

- *Projects.* A list describing school and personal projects (remember this is a brainstorm, a list is fine for now).

- *Professional Experience/Work Experience.* Work experience related to your field including part time, internships, and temporary positions.

- *Research.* Any help you have provided to a university research project.

- *Publications.* Papers, reports, or articles that have been made public from a respectable organization.

- *Skills.* A listing of tools, disciplines, and abilities which you have experience in. It is a good idea to categorize your skills into knowledge levels such as expert, knowledgeable, and intermediary.

- *Keywords.* This is a list of key terms and abbreviations that an employer is likely to use in a database search. This is only appropriate for a resume submitted online and often replaces the skills category.

- *Leadership.* Any positions or situations where you have led peers. For instance, situations where you have coordinated events, taken initiative in a social situation, or held a position in an organization are examples of leadership.

- *Honors/Awards.* Honors including academic awards, scholarships, and participation in relevant competitions.

- *Activities.* Anything you have been a part of related to your field. This includes events, competitions, conferences, seminars, talks, and clubs.

- *Interests/Additional.* Sometimes hobbies or interests can be what breaks the ice during an interview. For example, "Amateur Car Mechanic," may go a long way in showing that you are an engineer in many respects.

As an example fictitious candidate, Melissa Barnes will be going through the steps described in this chapter as well.

Some background on Melissa Barnes

Melissa is a sophomore computer engineering student. She considers herself an average student, but realized early that it is important to differentiate herself from other computer engineers. She has decided that cryptography and computer security interest her. Her goal is to get an internship for the National Security Agency (NSA).

Melissa also volunteers to help an animal clinic with their website. While volunteering she was introduced to the world of free open source software. The free tools she uses impressed her so much that she now keeps up with the news about them online (partially to help her keep the website up to date) and has even done a few bug fixes for the open source software she uses.

To illustrate the assembly of a content brainstorm into categories, here is what Melissa was able to come up with:

- *Objective*—To work on computer security as an intern

- *Education*—University of Washington, B.S. Computer Engineering, May, 2008, GPA 3.2

- *West Park animal clinic web master*—Quote from manager, designed web site from scratch, built with security in mind, automated appointment process, reduced operation costs, quote from Oregon Pet Magazine

- *Open Source*—Web Calendar mailing list quote, Web Calendar, phpMyAdmin, MySql, Apache, free BSD

- *Activities*—Seattle Secure World Expo, ACM programming competition, Society of Women Engineers, IEEE

- *Skills*—Mastery level skills: PHP, java script, web based authentication, C. Intermediate: C++, Java, perl, PKI. Additional: Linux, Unix, Apache, CVS

- *Interests*—Fencing, Volleyball, Cryptography

As you can see, Melissa has simply generated and organized her ideas deferring their development and the details for later. At this stage you should focus on *what* you want to include rather than *how* you will convey it.

NEXT, DEVELOP YOUR CONTENT CATEGORIES

This section covers the development of the initial content from the previous section. This includes how your ideas are to be expressed and formatted within a category. The "look and feel" or the visual development affecting the entire document such as fonts, category placement, and borders are covered in the next section.

When developing your ideas into complete thoughts, keep in mind that every line listed on your resume should be thought of as an advertisement. Concentrate on saying what is most important to the person that will read it. For example, if you are an assistant for a successful research project, "Research Assistant" is exactly what every other student who has helped a professor will put down on his or her resume. "Graphics Engine Architect" is far more interesting and descriptive. Did you design the whole thing yourself? No, but that is only the title to get their attention. Below the title you can explain that it was a university research project, which part of the system you designed, what you learned, and what the positive results were.

You may want to begin by developing an objective. An objective should not be taken lightly. It can have a powerful effect on where your resume ends up. Be as specific as possible if you choose to use an objective.

An objective such as, "Seeking an internship in mechanical engineering where I can be challenged" may suggest to a recruiter that you are giving them a generic resume and are not sure what you want to do within their organization. Doing a little bit of research on each company you send your resume to can go a long way. For example, "Objective: To improve the chassis engineering of Ford vehicles" could make a big difference. *Chapter 4: Researching an Organization* should be consulted when deciding on an objective.

When writing about accomplishments, keep in mind that the most crucial characteristic of a good resume is one that showcases a candidate's most important credentials after a fifteen second scan. Rules for writing essays and reports do not apply. Paragraphs go unread while bulleted lists or a hierarchy of headings can convey credentials quickly and clearly. The following example shows how ineffective a paragraph can be in a resume.

Paragraphs don't work in Resumes

Average Resume:

Computer Intern, June 2004—August 2004
I was responsible for troubleshooting and repairing computers at Electronics Plus as a part time job. We helped customers in person to plan a repair strategy and write up an estimate. I worked on over fifty computers and was often regarded as the best technician on the team. During the summer, the repair division of Electronic Plus increased its revenue by 23%. Management told me that I was a big part of their success.

Star Resume:

Computer Repair Consultant
Electronics Plus, Summer 2004

- Most talented computer technician from staff of eight professionals according to management

- Responsible for one-on-one consultation with clients to negotiate an estimate and repair plan

- Successfully troubleshooted and repaired over fifty personal computers

- Revenue increased by 23% which was directly attributed to my performance

When writing about major credentials such as projects and employment it is important to pick content that is the most relevant to an employer. Putting down whatever comes to mind regarding your part-time job may not be the best approach.

Each of your major accomplishments can be fully developed with the following three steps:

1. *Description of the endeavor.* A concise description of what you worked on is a requirement. It is common to see a laundry list of details regarding a job or

project; don't fall into this trap. Keep the description short and concentrate disproportionately on steps (2) and (3).

2. *Passion and an Industry Perspective.* As covered in *Chapter 1: Building Unmatched Credentials,* any indication that you have these characteristics differentiates you from your peers. Did the accomplishment get started or succeed due to a passion for your field? Did you take initiative where others failed? Did you gain knowledge or a practical skill that has enhanced your industry perspective?

3. *Results in a quantified form.* This is often overlooked and it is can make an enormous difference. Employers are very interested in how things turned out! Explain the results of the accomplishment and quantify those results with a fact or quote. Think of how you affected an organization or community and try to think of a way to prove the quality of your performance.

Consider this example which turns a routine resume accomplishment into one that shows passion, an industry perspective, and proven results.

From Assistant to Accomplished Engineer

Average Resume:

Engineering Assistant, Sept. 2003—Dec. 2003

- Johnson Engineers and Architects

- Auto Cad design. Structural calculations. Design of Paving, Grading, Drainage, Water and Sewer.

Star Resume:

Civil Engineer
Johnson Engineers and Architects, Fall 2003

- Designed 30,000 sq. ft. office building in record time

- Gained mastery in fundamental commercial civil engineering tech-niques:

  AutoCad design ♦ Structural analysis ♦ Paving
  Grading drainage ♦ Water ♦ Sewer design

- "Jeff is the most passionate young engineer I've met to date. His inno-vative design saved the company thousands of dollars"—Project Man-ager

Your choice of language can greatly influence the effectiveness of your resume. Here are some guidelines for fine-tuning your choice of words:

- *Simplicity always improves a resume.* Students tend to put as much jargon and details in their resume as possible. Clear descriptions in common language should come first and details second. A strong resume markets itself to anyone. When deciding on language, consider your grandparents; can they get the key information out of your statement?

- *Use powerful verbs at the beginning of each sentence fragment.* Strong verbs such as constructed, implemented, resolved, etc. market you as a motivated candi-date.

- *Focus on the core idea you are trying to convey to an employer.* Think about what you are really trying to say and cut the other details out. For example, "Researched a technique using curvature-based analysis of human heart data from a broad sample of patients using Fourier transforms and polynomial interpolation." should be replaced with "Invented a new technique for mea-suring the health of the human heart." The mathematical analysis used—Fou-rier transforms and polynomial interpolation—can be deferred to a skills section or a discussion in person.

Once you have revised your content brainstorm into fully developed accomplish-ments, it is a good idea to save your resume in a different file than what will become the final resume. This can be very handy when creating an online resume (covered in *Chapter 5: Secrets of Applying Online*) and as a basis for a new visual template as discussed in the next section.

Melissa Barnes spent the good part of an afternoon tinkering with her brainstorm and rewording accomplishments. If you remember, she is tailoring her content for an internship at the National Security Agency (NSA). Keep in mind that after making the transition from a brainstorm to developed content, you have completed a list of content categories with formal language, developed headings, and bulleted lists. So, this is not a complete resume yet (it still lacks visual formatting). Let's see what she came up with:

Developed content for Melissa Barnes

Objective
To better secure our country's assets using my knowledge of cryptography and technology

Education
University of Washington
B.S. Computer Engineering May, 2008
Overall GPA 3.2/4.0

Internet Technology Architect
West Park Animal Clinic, www.west-park-url.org,
November 2004—present
"Melissa has single handedly created new ways for our business to grow"—West Park owner

- Designed website using open source technology including:

  Public appointment calendar ◆ Personal record access

  Knowledge base ◆ Monthly newsletter from lead veterinarian

- Implemented the site with state-of-the-art computer security techniques:

  Advanced Apache configuration ◆ Router/firewall setup

  Modern web authentication ◆ Advanced Unix administration

- Featured as "*Best veterinary website for Seattle*"—*Oregon Pet Magazine, Jan. 2005*

Open Source Enthusiast
"*Nice work. We've been waiting for that bug fix for a while.*"–*WebCalendar mailing list*

- Open source developer and administrator
  Familiar with development and integration of industry leading open source programs, libraries and frameworks

- Contributor to:
  WebCalendar php online calendar,
  http://webcalendar.sourceforge.net
  phpMyAdmin data administration tool,
  http://phpmyadmin.sourceforge.net

- Configured and administer:
  MySql database system, http://mysql.org
  Apache web site server, http://apache.org
  FreeBSD Unix operating system, http://freebsd.org

Activities
Seattle Secure World Expo, October 2004
ACM programming competition, September 2004
Society of Women Engineers (SWE)
Institute of Electronic and Electrical Engineers (IEEE)

Skills
mastery level skills—C, PHP, javascript, web based authentication
intermediate—C++, Java, perl, PKI
additional—Linux, Unix, Code Versioning System (CVS)

Interests
Public key cryptography
Volleyball
Fencing

FINALLY, MAKE IT VISUALLY APPEALING

At this point your resume should have solid content; however, there are some additional things to be done in order to make it stand out when a hiring manager is flipping through a stack or to have it remembered after a long career event.

A resume contains a lot of information. It may not seem like a lot, but proportionate to how long it will be read, there is a lot to tell with no room for inefficiency. Fortunately, there are strategies for guiding your readers to the credentials they are most interested in as quickly as possible.

Think about other mediums that require navigation through a great deal of information. For example, a website of a large organization has a very well thought-out hierarchy. There is a menu system that allows you to find the page with the exact information you are looking for. The same applies in formatting your resume—make it easy. You have already started the process by converting the categories chosen in your brainstorm to first level headings. Bold/italic print, font size, and indentation are your tools for a hierarchy system. White space and borders are your tools for boxing in areas for people to focus on.

Here are some formatting ideas:

- *Bold text is not your only choice for headings.* A border below the text or surrounding the text can work well for a first level heading. The third resume of the upcoming samples serves as an example of this.

- *Maintain margins 0.6" or larger.* Reducing your margins is a great way to give you more flexibility when formatting your resume if you have a lot of content. For example, you can distribute the white space surrounding the document to areas surrounding sections that you want to emphasize. Of course, making the margins too small creates an unappealing visual affect.

- *Use a formal font between 10-12 pt.* A formal font such as Times Roman or Arial is recommended. Headings are an exception regarding size.

- *Take a step back to see if it's balanced.* It is visually appealing to have the text on the page weighted toward the center. If you fold it down the middle, both sides should have about the same amount of print.

- *Try using two columns if you are over one page.* Two columns increases the amount of content you can add to a single page. This can have amazing results on a previously two-page resume, but takes longer to format professionally.

- *Turn on hyphenation for your word processor.* This can save you lines and make the right margin look more balanced.

- *A picture is worth a thousand words (and words are in short supply).* A picture of yourself is not recommended; however, graphics such as logos representing the different places you have worked are often recognized instantly and can help to distinguish your resume.

There is no better way to learn how to make a resume visually appealing than by example. The profiles of rising stars provided at the end of each chapter conclude with the resume that landed them their dream job. In addition, the following resumes are excellent examples that you can use as templates. Our fictitious candidate, Melissa Barnes, is again used as a guinea pig.

Melissa Barnes

2701 NW 23rd Blvd, Apt. B91
Seattle, WA 98104

Phone: 206.333.7748
e-mail: mb@washington.edu

Objective

> To better secure our country's assets using my knowledge of cryptography and technology

Education

University of Washington   Seattle, WA
B.S. Computer Engineering May, 2008
Overall GPA 3.2/4.0

Internet Technology Architect

Nov. 2004 - present   West Park Animal Clinic, http://west-park-url.org   Bellevue, WA
"Melissa has single handedly created new ways for our business to grow" — owner
- Designed organizational website using open source technology including:
    Public appointment calendar • Personal record access
    Knowledge base • Monthly newsletter from lead veterinarian
- Implemented state-of-the-art computer security techniques. System includes:
    Advanced Apache configuration • Router/firewall setup
    Modern web authentication • Advanced Unix administration
- Featured as *"Best veterinary website for Seattle"* — *Oregon Pet Magazine, Jan. 2005*

Open Source Enthusiast

July 2003 - present   *"Nice work. We've been waiting for that bug fix for a while now." — WebCalendar mailing list*
- Open source developer and administrator. Familiar with compilation and integration
    of industry leading open source programs, libraries, and frameworks.
- Contributor to:
    WebCalendar php online calendar, http://webcalendar.sourceforge.net
    phpMyAdmin data administration tool, http://phpmyadmin.sourceforge.net
- Configure and administer:
    MySql database system, http://mysql.org
    Apache web site server, http://apache.org
    FreeBSD unix operating system, http://freebsd.org

Activities

- Seattle SecureWorld Expo, October 2004
- ACM programming competition, September 2004
- Society of Women Engineers (SWE)
- Institute of Electronic and Electrical Engineers (IEEE)

Skills

- *mastery level skills* — C, PHP, javascript, web based authentication
- *intermediate* — C++, Java, perl, PKI
- *additional* – Linux, Unix, Code Versioning System (CVS)

Interests

- Public key cryptography
- Volleyball
- Fencing

2701 NW 23ʳᵈ Blvd, Apt. B91   Phone: 206 333.7748
Seattle, WA 98104   e-mail: mb@washington.edu

Melissa Barnes

Objective

To better secure our country's assets using my knowledge of cryptography and technology

Education

Expected May 2008   Washington University   Seattle, WA
- B.S., Computer Engineering.
- Overall GPA 3.2/4.0

Internet Technology Architect

Nov. 2003–present   West Park Animal Clinic   Bellevue, WA
- *"Melissa has single handedly created new ways for our business to grow"* – owner
- Designed organizational website using open source technology including:
    Public appointment calendar ● Personal record access
    Knowledge base ● Monthly newsletter from lead veterinarian
- Implemented state-of-the-art computer security techniques. System includes:
    Advanced apache configuration ● Router/firewall setup
    Modern web authentication ● Advanced Unix administration
- Featured as *"Best veterinary website for Seattle"*
    – *Oregon Pet Magazine, January 2005*

Open Source Enthusiast

July 2002–present
- *"Nice work. We've been waiting for that bug fix for a while now."*
    – *WebCalendar mailing list*
- Open source developer and administrator
    Familiar with development and integration of industry leading open source programs, libraries, and frameworks
- Contributor to:
    WebCalendar php online calendar, http://webcalendar.sourceforge.net
    phpMyAdmin data administration, http://phpmyadmin.sourceforge.net
- Configured and administer:
    MySql database system, http://mysql.org
    Apache web site server, http://apache.org
    FreeBSD unix operating system, http://freebsd.org

Activities

- Seattle SecureWorld Expo, October 2004
- ACM programming competition, September 2004
- Society of Women Engineers (SWE)
- Institute of Electronic and Electrical Engineers (IEEE)

Skills

- *Mastery level skills* – C, PHP, javascript, web based authentication
- *Intermediate* – C++, Java, perl, PKI
- *Additional* – Linux, Unix, Code Versioning System (CVS)

Melissa Barnes

[phone] 206.333.7748
[e-mail] mb@washington.edu

2701 NW 23rd Blvd.
Seattle, WA, 98104

Objective

To better secure our country's assets using my knowledge of cryptography and technology

Education

University of Washington
B.S. Computer Engineering May, 2008
Overall GPA 3.2/4.0

Internet Technology Architect

West Park Animal Clinic, September 2003 – present
"Melissa has single handedly created new ways for our business to grow"—owner

- **Founded organizational web site using open source technology** (http://west-park-url.org)
  Includes public appointment calendar • Personal record access
  Knowledge base • Monthly newsletter from lead veterinarian
- **Exceeded requirements by devoting time to security**
  Includes advanced apache configuration • Router/firewall setup
  Modern web authentication • Advanced Unix administration
- **Renown locally as the best vet website in its market**

Open Source Enthusiast

"Nice work. We've been waiting for that bug fix for a while now."—WebCalendar mailing list

- **Open source developer and administrator with two years experience**
  Familiar with compilation and integration of industry leading open source programs, libraries, and frameworks:
    - *WebCalendar* Contributor to source (http://webcalendar.sourceforge.net)
    - *phpMyAdmin* Contributor to source (http://phpmyadmin.sourceforge.net)
    - *MySql* database system (http://mysql.org)
    - *Apache* web site server (http://apache.org)
    - *FreeBSD* unix operating system (http://freebsd.org)

Skills

- **Mastery level skills**—C, PHP, Javascript, web based authentication
- **Intermediate**—C++, Java, perl, PKI
- **Additional**—Linux, Unix, Code Versioning System (CVS)

Activities

Seattle SecureWorld Expo
ACM programming competition
Society of Women Engineers
Inst. of Electrical & Electronic Engineers

Interests

Public key cryptography
Volleyball
Fencing

THE CUSTOMIZABLE RESUME

Top candidates often tailor their resume for each job they apply for. This may seem like a lot of work, but with a little foresight changing 40% of your resume can be done in five minutes. If you want to take advantage of a customizable resume, expand your content brainstorm to include as broad a scope of accomplishments as possible. Don't just target one type of job; consider targeting roles you are more loosely qualified for. For instance, you may want to consider sales or consulting positions.

Once you have as broad of a content list as possible, you can create a template. Most word processors have the ability to create tables, columns, and complete document templates. Microsoft Word even comes with resume templates preinstalled. The second sample resume from the previous section was created with a Microsoft Word template.

Take advantage of these tools to create equally spaced areas where you can mix and match credentials. Customizing a resume can be as easy as pasting sections in and out from your content list or typing up a new category in a table cell to be saved for future use.

Below, the content for Melissa Barnes is expanded to include some additional credentials outside of security and software development. She has decided that she wants a customizable resume which she can use to target different disciplines of computer engineering.

Added content for Melissa Barnes

Group leader for assembly development

- Lead group of four which simulated 16-bit RISC processor

- First at university to use latest MIPS assembly version and compiler

- Exceeded requirements by simulating two processors in parallel

Implemented experimental database

- Designed for rapid development and reusability using Hibernate 3 beta

- Founder and evangelist for Hibernate's use at my university

Designed computer monitor driver

- Digital hardware circuit created with Altera software

- Ensured compatibility with the video graphics adapter standard (VGA)

- Quality of work is such that my personal computer uses the driver

Hardware position skill set

- Mastery level skills—Assembly, VHDL, C, PHP, javascript, cryptography

- Intermediate—VLSI, circuit board design, AutoCad, Pro/E, C++, Java, perl, PKI

- Additional—Digital design software, soldering, Linux, Unix

The following template is a resume Melissa has customized for a computer hardware position. She was able to build it by pasting different sections from her content list to predefined text areas in the template:

[phone] 206.333.7748
[e-mail] mb@washington.edu

Melissa Barnes

2701 NW 23rd Blvd.
Seattle, WA, 98104

Objective

To build the finest processor circuitry of our time using my expertise in analog and digital circuit design

Education

University of Washington
B.S. Computer Engineering May, 2008
Overall GPA 3.2/4.0

Projects

Designed computer monitor driver circuit

- Digital hardware circuit created with Altera software
- Insured compatibility with the video graphics adapter standard (VGA)
- Quality of work is such that my personal computer uses the driver

Group leader for assembly development

- Lead group of four to simulate 16-bit RISC processor
- First at university to use latest MIPS assembly spec and compiler
- Exceeded requirements by simulating two processors in parallel

Professional Experience

West Park Animal Clinic, September 2003 – present
"Melissa has single handedly created new ways for our business to grow"—owner

- **Founded organizational web site using open source technology** (http://west-park-url.org)
  Includes public appointment calendar • Personal record access
  Knowledge base • Monthly newsletter from lead veterinarian
- **Exceeded requirements by devoting time to security** from the ground up
  Includes advanced apache configuration • Router/firewall setup
  Modern web authentication • Advanced Unix administration
- **Renown locally as the best vet website in its market**

Skills

- **Mastery level skills**—Assembly, VHDL, C, PHP, javascript, cryptography
- **Intermediate**—VLSI, circuit board design, AutoCad, Pro/E, C++, Java, perl, PKI
- **Additional**—Digital design software, soldering, Linux, Unix

Activities

Seattle SecureWorld Expo
ACM programming competition
Society of Women Engineers
Inst. of Electrical & Electronic Engineers

Interests

Public key cryptography
Volleyball
Fencing

FEEDBACK FROM OTHERS CAN MAKE THE DIFFERENCE

Does your resume clearly state your key credentials? Does it look professional? Does it reflect all of your strengths? Does it represent your personality and style? All of these questions can be answered with feedback from others.

It can be difficult to be objective when you are being criticized about something you have worked hard on. You certainly don't have to take someone else's advice, but never discourage someone from stating his or her opinion. Keep this in mind—if someone looks at your resume and finds something to be unclear or undesirable, it is very likely there is a hiring manager out there that shares the same view.

Don't make a change every time you get a recommendation either, you will hear all sorts of opinions which often conflict. There is no perfect solution. Recruiters and hiring managers do not think the same; in fact their opinions of candidates are incredibly diverse. For instance, in the end, it is your choice whether you want to be conservative, so you look professional to as broad an audience as possible, or to be a little bold in an effort to differentiate yourself.

When you seek feedback, be sure to test your resume's effectiveness within a fifteen second time-frame whenever possible. Hand it to your critiquer and tell them to scan it for fifteen seconds. Once the time is up, ask them to explain everything they have learned about you. What credentials they recall over others can be surprising. If you have to pry out the most important accomplishments, then your resume isn't doing its job.

In order to facilitate gathering feedback, you may want to hand out copies of your resume to be marked up with suggestions. Just about anyone can assist in your review including family, friends, professors, college career advisors, etc. It is wise to record all comments in one place, especially suggestions which affect the entire document such as font or white space changes. This way when you are done collecting feedback you can review all the aggregated suggestions before making decisions.

THE BARE MINIMUM TO DO

How you write your resume is up to you. This chapter is only here to give you ideas and some guidelines to help you through the process. What if you only have a few days before a career event? Below is the bare minimum to run through and some estimates of how much time to set aside.

1. *Brainstorm content (30 min).* Start with an old resume or transcripts of the classes you have taken and write down whatever comes to mind.

2. *Narrow down your brainstorm and choose categories (10 min).* Pick out the best categories from those listed earlier in this chapter to best showcase your credentials.

3. *Develop your accomplishments into paragraphs (1 hr).* Keep things simply, clear, and remember that you are writing advertisements. Show passion, an industry perspective, and quantified results wherever possible.

4. *Use two levels of headings, bulleted lists, and action words (30 min).* Convert the paragraphs into labeled and easily accessed information.

5. *Use a good template (1 hr).* Paste your developed content into a word processor template or use one of the formats illustrated in the sample resumes or the resumes provided in the profiles appended to each chapter.

6. *Seek feedback from anyone and everyone (2+ days).* Spend the rest of your time talking to people about your resume. Be sure to replicate its real job by having it scanned for no longer than fifteen seconds. The rest of your available time should be spent on feedback and incremental editing.

COMMON MISTAKES

1. *Typos and spelling.* This can land your resume in the trash. Do whatever it takes to avoid grammatical errors.

2. *Personal information.* Personal details such as age, sex, weight, and religion should be avoided.

3. *Unprofessional style.* Elegant is good, but flashy and obnoxious is bad. Avoid colors, large irrelevant graphics, and unconventional fonts.

4. *Too long.* Even if you have four internships, do not go over a page in a college resume. If you are a graduate student that has worked full-time in the past, then two pages should be your absolute maximum.

5. *Listing classes.* Recruiters and hiring managers have access to the curriculum and will ask for transcripts if this is not the case. Listing classes is like stating that you graduated from high school—everyone has done it.

6. *Descriptions of duties and responsibilities.* If you are copying lengthy official job descriptions you are wasting valuable space. An accomplishment-oriented resume is a far better advertisement.

7. *Personal pronouns such as Me, I, and My.* They can often be avoided and it is always an improvement to do so.

8. *Failure to use word processor properly.* If something seems tedious, look in the help system for the correct way to do it. A common mistake is to use consecutive spaces or tabs when margin alignments or tables can save headaches. Poor formatting can ruin your chances if your resume is e-mailed to a recruiter. It may be converted to a different format or an older version of the word processor may be in use. If poor formatting techniques are used, the resume can display imporperly.

9. *Does not photocopy well.* Sometimes fancy paper and ink can do more harm than good. Keep in mind that if an employer is interested, your resume will be photocopied up to a dozen times.

10. *Listing references.* Leave out references. You should write, "References available upon request" only if you need something to balance out the document.

Profile
Jay Ayres

Who do you work for, what is your official internship title, and where is it located?

I work for Autodesk Inc.'s Geographic Information Systems division as a Software Development Intern. The job is located in Ithaca, NY.

Was it your first choice?

Absolutely. Autodesk is a highly-regarded software company that has an office quite close by to Cornell University, where I attend school, so relocation wasn't necessary for me.

What are some positive aspects of the internship?

I feel like I have learned a lot in my current position, which has been essential for me since this is my first real technical internship. I've been able to learn new technologies such as C#, the .NET Framework, and Windows Mobile development, and have also learned a lot about software development methodologies such as Extreme Programming. I've also honed my technical writing skills by documenting all of the work I've done. Finally, I've gained some experience with software testing, mostly through the form of finding/fixing bugs and using automated test scripts.

What are some negative aspects?

As an intern, my role has been mainly to write software according to specifications designed by others. When I look for a full-time position, I hope to have the responsibility of actually designing software specifications. With concerns in this industry about offshoring, software engineers such as myself cannot be content simply being code monkeys anymore.

What is your typical day like?

I come into the office at around 8 AM, and typically leave no later than 5 PM, with a 30-minute break for lunch. Most projects I work on are 2-3 day-long ventures into writing a new software feature or fixing a bug, but I always spend some time each day looking for new bugs based on the previous night's software build.

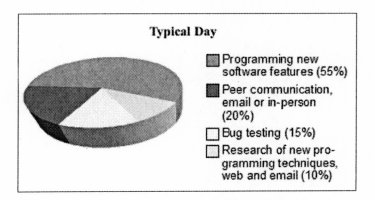

How did you make initial contact with Autodesk?

Cornell University's co-op program brought many employers to campus who explicitly were looking for current college sophomores to spend a semester working for their company. I submitted my resume to Autodesk via the co-op program's website.

I applied in the fall which I think increased my chances a lot. Many companies have just as much work to do during the Spring and Fall semesters as the summer and fewer student apply during those periods. Something else that made the difference was doing some company research. After looking over their website, I was able to find out that division of Autodesk in Ithica was originally a Cornell startup. I later found out that I was the only candidate to interview that knew this.

Did you tailor your resume for the position?

I rearranged my coursework and experience to match their needs which I knew would be C++ programming. I was sure to include soft skills such as my social activity in a fraternity as well. I highly recommend tailoring an objective toward every position you apply for.

What advice do you have for someone working on their resume?

Detail your experiences rather then just putting them in a bulleted list. If you've taken an engineering class, talk about the tools and projects from the class rather then listing the course number.

Use action verbs wherever possible such as constructed, provided, created, etc. If you list a skill, make sure you can expand on it and are fairly knowledgeable on the subject. You don't want to get caught as a resume padder. If your resume is very focused on your field, you may want to add some soft skills to show you are socially adept and a good communicator.

What were your interviews like?

I actually only had one thirty-minute interview, most likely because of restrictions placed on the employers by Cornell's co-op program. It was 50% behavioral and 50% technical. It was my first real experience with a job interview, being that I was only a sophomore in college.

Have any memorable questions?

Luckily, I didn't get any "Why are manhole covers round?" types of questions, but rather I got straightforward questions about C++ and Java. They asked me at the end, "Is there anything else you'd like to tell us about yourself?" and I always like to use that opportunity to highlight an item on my resume that has not already come up. I often like to speak of my involvement in a fraternity in college, because it shows that I have taken on leadership roles in the past and am not someone who is chained to a computer all of the time!

Note: At the time of this book's publication, Jay Ayres completed his internship at Autodesk. He went on to graduate school at Stanford University.

Kenneth J. ("Jay") Ayres, Jr.

School Address:
207 Running Farm Lane, #105
Stanford, CA 94305
Tel. # (607) 731-0151

Email Address: jayres@stanford.edu

Home Address:
21 Infield Ct. North
Rockville, MD 20854
Tel. # (301) 294-0995

Objective:
To obtain a full-time development position that leverages my experience in enterprise technology.

Education:
Stanford University
> Master of Science in Computer Science, completion date December 2005

Cornell University
> Graduated Magna Cum Laude from the College of Engineering, June 2004
>
> Bachelor of Science in Computer Science, with a minor in Operations Research and Industrial Engineering
>
> Cumulative GPA: 3.914 on a 4.3 scale (3.96 major GPA)
>
> Cornell Presidential Research Scholars; McMullen Book Award; Dean's List 7 out of 8 semesters

Experience:
IBM (Austin, TX   6/04-8/04)
> Designed a platform to stream images from an advanced graphics processor to handheld devices in real time, creating the illusion that 3D rendering is done on the handheld itself. This project was part of IBM's Extreme Blue internship program.

Autodesk (Ithaca, NY 6/03-8/03)
> Ported the source code for Autodesk Envision™, a geographic information systems application, from Windows to the PocketPC using the .NET Compact Framework and eMbedded Visual C++.

Autodesk (Ithaca, NY 8/02-1/03)
> Implemented new features and found/fixed bugs for Autodesk OnSite Desktop™ using Visual C# and the Microsoft .NET Framework. This project was part of Cornell's Engineering Co-op program.

Coursework/Projects:
> Web Services, Database Systems, Computer Networks, Systems Programming, Compilers, Computer Graphics, Computer Organization, Analysis of Algorithms, Probability & Statistics, Information Technology, Engineering Communications
>
> Research in the field of database systems as part of the Cornell Database group:
> - Helped design and implement a routing protocol in Java for networked wireless devices to retrieve and aggregate sensor data in an energy-efficient manner
> - Wrote an algorithm in C++ to find frequent sequential patterns in transactional databases

Publications:
> Jay Ayres, J. E. Gehrke, Tomi Yiu, and Jason Flannick. Sequential PAttern Mining Using Bitmaps. In *Proceedings of the Eighth ACM SIGKDD International Conference on Knowledge Discovery and Data Mining.* Edmonton, Alberta, Canada, July 2002 (28.6% paper acceptance rate)

Special Skills:
> Familiarity with J2EE development (EJB, JSP, Struts, JBoss, Eclipse, XDoclet, Ant)
> Project experience with Java, C++, C, Windows CE, SQL, Perl
> Experience in industry working with the .NET Framework (C#, managed C++, ASP, ADO.NET)

Activities/Interests:
> Tau Beta Pi Engineering Honor Society; I do tutoring and community service with this organization
> Brother of Acacia Fraternity; have held positions as scholarship chair and alumni affairs chair

3

Writing a Strong Cover Letter

A cover letter is a brief one page letter that accompanies your resume. It is an introduction of the candidate to the employer. It serves for a single purpose—to convince a hiring manager or recruiter to read your resume. A good cover letter explains why the candidate is a perfect fit for the job clearly and concisely.

A well-written cover letter is next in line behind a good resume for increasing a candidate's potential in the shortest period of time. This chapter explains how a cover letter can serve you well and provides guidelines to writing a strong cover letter. Additionally, it should save you from common pitfalls in putting together college cover letters.

It is recommended that you look over *Chapter 4: Researching an Organization* and *Chapter 2: Crafting a Successful Resume* before you begin writing cover letters. Knowing key information about an organization is essential for introducing yourself to employers in writing and a cover letter shares a significant amount of content with a resume.

WHY COVER LETTERS ARE IMPORTANT

A strong cover letter can create opportunities for you that otherwise would not exist. Being a formal document, it can be sent to nearly any division of an organization—not just to an online career website. A strong cover letter can easily travel into the hands of a manager who is considering to hire someone new, but has not gotten around to making arrangements with their human resource department.

If the letter and enclosed resume are in line with the manager's needs, it is likely that he or she will move mountains to create an opportunity even if there were no plans to hire anyone previously. Thus, a well crafted cover letter can grant you exclusive access to a manager outside of conventional recruiting channels. This is more common than you may think—over two thirds of professional job openings in the United States are not listed publicly before a decision is made.

A formal cover letter can be sent to any address, including e-mail addresses. For example, take a company's customer service department. A plain resume sent to such an address is likely to be tossed aside. However, a cover letter beginning with "I had the most fascinating conversation yesterday with one of your representatives" could result in your letter being circulated among all the managers in the department. If nothing else, the organization will be complemented that you are so interested in them that you've put together a pleasant, formal letter just for them.

A cover letter is your chance to make the case that you are the best fit for an open position. The letter is an opportunity to showcase your best and most relevant credentials. It allows you to outline why you're a strong candidate.

Additionally, it allows you to explain credentials and situations that a resume cannot. For example, if you are in an unusual degree program that few universities offer, you can explain the curriculum and how it makes you a unique candidate in your cover letter. Another example is an explanation for a long break before or during college.

Finally, a cover letter shows that you can write well. Communication is arguably a universal requirement of college positions. Hiring managers often read cover letters solely to find out how well you organize and convey information.

WHAT TO FOCUS ON

It can be tempting to start by opening a text editor and writing what comes to mind—avoid it. The first step should always be finding out about the employer. The more you know about the position or group, the better you can match your credentials to what they are hiring for. It is recommended that you consult *Chapter 4: Researching an Organization*.

Once you have a clear understanding of what you are applying for and what the needs are for that position, it is helpful to organize your draft into sections. Here is what is recommended:

- *Heading.* This section includes everything before the first paragraph. It should include the date, the address for whom you are sending it to, your address, and a greeting. Try to use a name for someone within the organization for the greeting, for example "Dear Ms. Williamson:" When in doubt about a name or proper greeting, always try to call someone in the organization such as a receptionist or assistant. If you are unsure of the gender of the recipient, write out the full name. In the case where you are not able to get the name of someone within the organization, "Attention Recruiting Coordinator:" is appropriate.

- *Introduction.* Your introduction needs to explain why your letter is relevant to their organization, why you are writing them, and who you are. If you have an objective on your resume tailored for the employer, it may be appropriate to mention it again here.

- *Argument.* This is where you make your case to the employer. Concentrate on how you can add value to their organization, not just your accomplishments. If you have a specialty within your field which is relevant, be sure to mention your passion for the related department or product line of the organization. Try to keep it under three paragraphs; assume your reader is busy and won't read every word.

- *Closing.* Your closing statement should summarize your argument and finish on a positive note. Don't be afraid to request an interview in your closing; it shows initiative. It is also appropriate to leave your preferred contact information.

Be sure that your letter is error free. Otherwise, your efforts to write a professional, formal document have failed. It is very difficult to properly proofread a document immediately after writing it. Once you have a draft together, wait at least a day before sending it. If you can't wait, have someone else proofread it.

Once you have written a few cover letters, it will become much easier to produce tailored letters for every employer you apply to. You'll have a good starting point and structure to build from.

TEN COVER LETTER TIPS

Here are some other pointers which will make your cover letter a pleasure to read. Be sure to go over the common mistakes section as well.

1. *Keep it brief.* Try to stay within four paragraphs and be sure to never go over a single page. Too short can be a poor decision as well. The minimum should be three paragraphs (i.e. introduction, argument, closing).

2. *Use simple language.* A journalist in training is often taught to "write tight," because it is believed that people are more likely to read articles which are written concisely and with simplicity rather than elaborate language (writing tight also saves valuable space in publications). It is the recommendation of this book to do the same—make it easy.

3. *Make sure the first paragraph generates attention.* Motivate the reader to keep reading! Be creative, passionate, and insightful about their business. Avoid vague language and anything that sounds overdone.

4. *Be sure to address your letter to a person if possible.* It makes it look a lot more like a letter you have written just for that organization. As it gets circulated to different people, it will stand out if it is addressed to someone familiar.

5. *Use a serif font from ten to twelve points in size.* It is not the time to be flashy or creative when it comes to formatting. A twelve point sans serif font such as Times Roman or Courier is standard and formal. Also, serif fonts are proven to be easier to read as opposed to sans serif fonts (such as Arial which does not have typewriter style edges).

6. *Summarize the purpose within each paragraph at the beginning.* Have you ever studied the way you scan a page of text in a hurry? You probably glance at the first few sentences of a paragraph and skip it if you are not immediately interested. Be sure the first sentence of a paragraph represents the rest properly.

7. *Focus on them rather than you.* Show that you have researched the company and can talk a bit about the organization—not just your goals. Just listing the best parts of your resume is not very productive. Try explaining why your accomplishments are relevant to the position.

8. *Sign it in ink.* This is a requirement to make it look formal and professional. If you are submitting a cover letter electronically, scan your signature and insert it as an image.

9. *Use wide margins.* 1 to 1.25 inches is standard for a letter. If you are tempted to reduce the margins, your cover letter is far too long.

10. *Center the letter vertically.* A centered document is visually appealing and professional. ·

EXAMPLE COVER LETTERS

The following fictitious letters should provide a great way to get started. They illustrate the simple plan of using an introduction, argument, and closing clearly. Additionally, the letters show how effective good research and a focus on how the candidate will help the employer can be. These letters would certainly serve as a powerful tool for their respective authors—creating custom employment opportunities which do not exist on public listings.

Kenneth Donald
283 Westford Dr.
Buffalo, NY 14202
(352) 234-2352

March 5th, 2005

Richard J. Johnson
General Motors Co.
100 Renaissance Center
Detroit, MI 48243

Dear Mr. Johnson:

Professor William K. Clark of my university recommended that I contact you since my specialty is also in manufacturing tool design. My research experience and industry knowledge in large-scale manufacturing tools should be a strong match for your team and GM's industry leading manufacturing process.

In various capacities in engineering with academically recognized research at my university, leading to professional industry experience with The Toro Company in Minnesota, I have acquired skills in all phases of manufacturing tool design including computer aided modeling, ordering custom materials, shop assembly, and quality assurance.

I am sure that I can contribute to your success after my degree is complete in early May. I will be visiting Detroit on April 15th and would appreciate the opportunity to showcase how I can help GM's production tool team meet its goals.

Sincerely,

Kenneth Donald

101 NW 4th Ave.
Tucson, AZ 85749
November, 20th 2005

Joan L. Chen
Adobe Systems Inc.
801 N. 34th Street
Seattle, WA 98103

Dear Dr. Chen:

I was fortunate enough to hear you speak during the 2004 XML Exposition in Washington, DC and was amazed to find your work is exactly in line with my research. My knowledge and passion for electronic document interoperability within an enterprise setting would be invaluable to the Adobe Intelligent Document Platform.

From very early on in college, I have felt that the enormous resources companies use to manually read paper forms which require actions such as phone calls and e-mails will be replaced by powerful documents that both humans and computers can read.

This vision has lead to my involvement in a variety of fascinating pet projects and online contributions in the realm of business processes and XML. My co-op experience with McKechnie & Bernard LLC, a rapidly growing mortgage firm, has given me the freedom to design a company-wide conversion from paper processes to workflows driven by documents represented with XML. The mid-size business has seen a significant improvement in operating costs due to the elimination of paper forms and e-mail which previously required manual action.

I'll be completing my degree in Computer Science in mid-December and would like to discuss how I can bring great value to your team. It would also be fascinating to hear more of your insights on how organizations are fundamentally changing to be driven by documents—not deterred by them. You can reach me at 520-235-0921.

Sincerely,

David A. Winters

COMMON MISTAKES

1. *Typos and spelling.* You may notice that this tops the common mistakes list for resumes as well. Again, do whatever it takes to avoid grammatical errors.

2. *Clichés such as "Enclosed please find my resume."* Take initiative and create your own well-written language. In this case, it makes little sense to state that a resume is enclosed. Cover letters have become so common place that employers will expect an attached resume.

3. *Addressing the recipient by first name.* Unless you know them personally, it is impolite.

4. *Slang.* In an effort to keep your language simple, natural, and concise you may have included slang on accident. It can brand you as a poor communicator.

5. *Constant use of "I."* Most sentences can be reworded so they do not begin with "I." For example, "I worked at a chemistry lab freshman year" can be reworded as "During my freshman year, I worked at a chemistry lab." Also, try to replace statements about your personal goals and accomplishments with statements of value specific to the employer.

6. *A generic letter.* Recruiters will see a canned letter from a mile away. Tailor your introduction and argument for each employer.

7. *Missing date, address, or contact information.* Employers often keep records of contact information from applicants. No phone number or e-mail address will certainly hinder your chances.

8. *Mentioning personal reasons for seeking the position.* If you are tempted to mention how much your cat, Titan, desperately needs to live in a warmer climate, restrain yourself. It can be beneficial to express that you are truly interested in working for an employer, but leave personal reasons out.

9. *Mentioning salary expectations.* This is far too early to be negotiating salary. Your ethics and honest interest in the organization may be questioned. If you don't want to interview unless they are in your salary range ask yourself if it's worth eliminating all hope (besides passing up interviewing experience should never be done). Unfortunately, there is no way to know an

employer's ultimate flexibility in salary until you have the leverage of success-fully completed interviews. Salary negotiation will be explained in *Chapter 10: Understanding Human Resources–HR interviews, salary negotiation, & more.*

10. *Anything negative.* Think of your cover letter as your resume's personal little cheerleader. Avoid anything that is passive and negative such as "Currently, I'm not really sure if your company would be the best fit, but…"

Profile
Szymon Swistun

Who do you work for, what is your official internship title, and where is it located?

I work as an intern for the games division of EA Tiburon, a studio of Electronic Arts in Orlando, Florida that develops sports and action video games.

Was it your first choice?

Definitely. I was also considering a position with Microsoft and a smaller video game development company called Budcat Creations. It was an interesting decision between two large stable companies and a startup of fourteen people. I think Budcat would have allowed me to have more influence over the final product which was appealing.

What are some positive aspects of the internship?

First and foremost, I write video games. In deciding on a career path I realized that the most important aspect of a job for me over compensation, culture, or other attributes is how passionate I feel about it. My passion lies in animation, 3-D graphics, and game development in general so I don't think I could find a better job.

Additionally, the work environment I'm in is very open. I can talk to senior developers whenever I'm curious. It's an awesome team environment with camaraderie—everyone works together. It's as if everyone feeds off each other's energy.

I have to admit that Orlando is a great location as well—you can't go wrong with Florida.

What are some negative aspects?

One drawback for the gaming industry in general is that product development is cyclical. Most of the time we work 40-50 hours a week, but a few months out of the year 70-80 hours is the norm. It is a consumer driven industry. For example, football games need to be available before the football season starts. EA is very good about releasing their products on time.

What is your typical day like?

I get into work around 10 AM. After I'm settled, I begin work on specific deliverables that have been set for the week. I work in a group of about seven people and am constantly talking and bouncing ideas off my teammates. Once a week we have a status meeting where new work is divided among groups and I find out what the other groups are up to.

Before lunch, my team likes to have a session of about thirty minutes where we just goof off. We have some juggling balls that we find innovative uses for, relax, and generally mess around.

We always go out for lunch. Lunch is usually around 12:30 and lasts about 45 minutes. When I get back, I like to grab a coke from the on-site vending machines where everything is a quarter.

After lunch I continue working on my deliverables and sometimes focus my attention on a critical report from another team that has questions about the in-house game development tools I help write. My activities usually break down as follows:

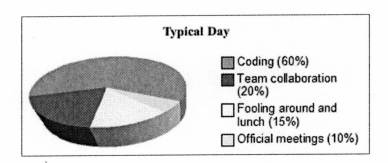

I usually leave around 6-7 PM. Although, there was one day where I stayed until midnight helping with the installation of a new code versioning system. I was humbled by the fact that someone ranked far above me gave me the job of overseeing its installation considering I'm just an intern. I was promptly rewarded for staying late by getting the next day off.

How did you make initial contact with EA?

EA has an online recruiting system that stores a profile of your skills, resume, cover letter, etc. The system sends an email when your profile matches an available position. I received an email inviting me to take an online test. The test was written by the EA Tiburon studio. I think the style of the test depends a lot on the division it is for. I then received an email congratulating me for doing well on the test and an invitation for a phone interview. I received an HR screening interview and later a technical interview which was a phone conference with three developers. Finally, I was flown to Orlando for a site interview.

Something interesting that happened in my case was that when my online profile matched for a job, it matched me with a senior software developer position. I wasn't sure what to do since I didn't want to lose an opportunity. So, I decided to take the senior test and managed to pass it. When I had my screening interview they started to ask me about previous experience qualifying me to be a senior developer and I had to explain that I'm just a sophomore in college looking for an internship.

What were your site interviews like?

It started out with a nice lunch with three directors. Afterwards I had a two hour written test. The site interview consisted of 60% behavioral, 25% technical, and 15% HR related questions.

Have any memorable questions?

You have a game that is running slow—lets say at 20 frames per second. You have tasks that the game must perform which have already been written to be as fast as possible such as AI that takes X cycles, rendering that takes Y cycles, and keyboard input which takes Z cycles. How do you increase the frame rate of the game?

My solution was to keep rendering on at all times, but interleave the other tasks. For example, you probably don't need AI to run on every frame—it could run every other frame. In theory, I made a trade-off between quality and performance, but in practice it could be done so the user doesn't even notice the difference in quality.

There is another question that comes to mind from an NVIDIA interview. I was asked to write an "aligned malloc" function and its corresponding "free" function. If you are a C programmer you know how insane this question is. I was not prepared to answer it in less than an hour's time. In other words, it destroyed me.

What advice do you have for writing cover letters?

Tailor your cover letter for a position. It is important to write a genuine letter, those hiring will notice and appreciate the difference. Make yourself an appealing candidate for the position. If it's an entry level position show that you are humble and looking forward to learning from the rest of the team with more experience, but have aspirations to do some amazing things in the future.

200 Colonial Homes Dr. apt 1204   gtg157a@mail.gatech.edu
Atlanta, GA 30309   (404) 512-4062

Szymon Swistun

Objective

To gain an internship position within a competitive, fast-paced electronic game development environment.

Work Experience

June 2002 – Present   **Georgia Tech Research Institute**
Atlanta, GA

- **Augmented Reality Client Side Software Developer**
- Currently a member of a team responsible for the development of the first 3D multi-user game designed for AR Technology using Macromedia Director MX and DART VRPN dev tools.

May 2003 – August 2003   **Electronic Arts – Tiburon**
Maitland, FL

- **Software Development Intern**
- Extended EA Worldwide's development tool (In-Game Flash movie module) to function within the XBOX using Microsoft's XBOX development station and MS XDK.
- Headed the development of a comprehensive unit-testing module and testing harness in C++ for future Tiburon tool application and in-game unit-testing integration.
- Enhanced Tiburon's main animation backbone to operate alongside multiple source control providers such as Visual Source Safe, Perforce and Alien Brain.

June 2000 – October 2000   **Integrated Software Specialists**
Schaumburg, IL

- **General Intern, Recruiter, Software Engineer**
- Assumed increasing responsibility in a software engineering position and coded Java applets with Visual Café 4.0 and Java 1.2.

Personal Experience

- Currently developing a 3D OpenGL C++ game engine that will integrate per pixel shading, bump and gloss mapping, quaternion based animation, and an innovative time based network architecture. (http://www.swigged.net/dreadcity/)
- Produced two "real" physics modifications of Quake 3 that transformed the system's infrastructure allowing a more dynamic client to client communication along with innovative battling systems.
- Extensive programming experience with DirectX 8.0, OpenGL, GLUT 3.7, XBOX XDK, PS2 ProDG, .Net 2003, MS VC++ 6.0, MFC, STL, Perforce, VSS, CVS, UML, Rational Rose, Visio, 3DSMAX 2.5, Maya 4.0, Java 1.4, Java 3D, Linux, DOM, SAX, XML, Smalltalk, and ANSI C.

Education

2001-2003   Georgia Institute of Technology   Atlanta, GA

- **B.S., Computer Science Candidate**, May 2005. GPA: 3.22/4.0   Dean's List
  - Coded an OO Model / Camera script based 3D OpenGL animation engine in C++.
  - Developed a multi-threaded 3D Network version of Go in Java with 3 teammates.
  - Single-handedly developed a comprehensive compiler in ANSI C.

Activities

- Member, Tau Kappa Epsilon Fraternity. (Information Technology Chairman, 2002)
- Georgia Tech Success Center and Athletic Association CS1322 Java programming tutor.
- Georgia Tech Varsity Mascot "Buzz". (2001 – 2003)
- Competed with the Midwest Water Polo Zone Team at the Senior Men's National Water Polo Tournament in the summer of 2000 at Irvine, Texas.
- Participated with NIPC at the Junior Olympics of 2000 in Orange County, California.

4

Researching an Organization

Company research is the most under-utilized step in making the transition from college to a career. It seems that most job seekers see it as an optional activity compared to crafting a resume or attending a career fair. You may be thinking "It will take me too much time to do research and I don't think it can make a difference in the end." It turns out that smart research can have a big impact on whether you ultimately land your dream job. Being well informed will help you to tailor your resume, cover letter, and give you the foundation for engaging conversations with employers.

Research isn't necessarily time consuming and without recognizable results either. The key to company research is defining criteria ahead of time. Compare building a research plan to writing a shopping list—it gives you set goals to accomplish, saves you time, and makes sure all your needs are covered. Once some goals are set, navigating the wealth of information available becomes less complex and more rewarding.

This chapter explains how good research can help you at every stage of landing the job. It also defines what to look for and where to find sources of information.

REASONS TO DO COMPANY RESEARCH

Information you gather about an employer should be used throughout your transition from college to a career. Here are some ways research can help you land the job:

- *By helping you find a specialty.* Specializing within your field is important during college as described in "Choosing a topic of interest in your field" in Chapter 1. Smart company research can help you determine current company strategy and areas of growth within an industry. For example, Voice over Internet Protocol (VoIP) is a rapidly growing technology within the telecommunications industry. Company research can help break down a company into its departments and divisions which specialize in various areas. One of these areas may serve as an interesting specialty.

- *By providing information to map your skills to a business.* Knowing exactly what skills a department or group within a company needs is critical in differentiating yourself in a cover letter, in a resume, or during an interview. For example, imagine that you are in the middle of an HR interview over the phone with the company and are asked "What do you want to do?" A typical response, which any HR representative is used to hearing, may sound like "I'm looking for a challenging position in Electrical Engineering." However, a candidate that has done some smart company research may reply with "If I'm not mistaken, your GPT division is moving from analog components to digital components. My specialty is in digital design control logic so I think I could add great value to the transition."

- *By helping you determine if the company is a strong fit for you.* Choosing a company is very much like choosing a university. Companies vary in culture, size, location, and policy. Finding out if a company is in line with your expectations is important to help you make the right choice for your future. Additionally, "Why do you want to work for us?" is almost universally asked by employers. Showing that you understand the organization's culture and have an honest response explaining why you fit into that culture can be impressive.

- *By providing key information before a career event or interview.* Imagine that you are interviewing for a position and you are familiar with the department the interviewer works under. The interviewer is impressed and you begin a brief discussion over that department's role within the company. Your research has allowed you to begin the interview with an engaging conversation where you are comfortable and confident. That alone may land you the job. Company research can give you valuable knowledge to draw upon when having conversations with employers.

WHAT YOU NEED TO FIND OUT

Before randomly reading magazine articles and company career websites it is best to set some goals determining what needs to be researched. This section will help you come up with a plan so you can spend your time searching for specific information.

The best approach is to start with broad company information and then narrow your focus on a particular department, product, or location of the company. Once you have a specific area of the business to target, it is more manageable to become knowledgeable on the area. Suggestions for research criteria are discussed in this section at a bird's eye view first. Then, criteria appropriate for a specific target is covered.

How much time it takes to be informed on your target depends on the nature of the company and how well informed you want to be. The suggestions in this section (and in this chapter for that matter), err on the side of more information to provide a complete picture of the possibilities. If you were to employ every suggestion in this chapter for every organization you are even loosely considering, you could very well unexpectedly extend your time in college. The reader is encouraged to build a research plan that fits his or her needs and goals. Additionally, if you are short on time, be sure to look over *"The Bare Minimum To Do."*

Broad Criteria

One method of clearly defining goals for company research is to make a list of questions. Here are some high-level questions to consider:

- *What products or services does the company provide?* This is essential to research. You may think "I can skip this, I know company XYZ makes toasters." Be careful, companies often have more then one product line. For example, in addition to toasters, the company may also own a manufacturer of aerospace parts for government contracts. Try to collect an overview of the company's entire portfolio of products and services—even those which are not as successful.

- *Is it a large, mid-size, or small business?* Company size ranges from a single owner to over a million employees (Wal-Mart Stores was the largest corporation in 2004 with 1,007,509 employees according to Fortune Magazine).

Company size can be determined by various statistics including the number of employees, revenue, market share, etc. The number of employees within a company is probably most notable. A small company is usually under 2,000 employees and large company can be categorized as having more than 15,000 employees.

- *How is the company organized?* This includes divisions by product, services, technology, industry, and region. A good way to start is to find out how the management of the organization is divided. For example, you may want to find out who the top officers are that lead research, production, sales, marketing, finance, and human resources. Another way to research company organization is by investigating each location and corporate office. Ideally, although difficult for many organizations, it should be broken down until you are looking at a subset of groups totaling less than a few hundred people.

- *Who is the competition?* Reading about the competition and finding the advantages a company has over competitors can provide valuable insight. Researching a company's market share is also useful. Market share is the percentage of revenue a company makes compared to the total revenue gained by its entire market. For example, AMD saw its market share rise to 15.8 percent in late 2004, according to Mercury Research.

- *What partners does the company leverage?* A partner is an organization that has made a long-term agreement to help a company because of common interests. For example, a partner may provide quality assurance experts to make sure a company's products meet customer requirements in exchange for accounting services. Partners can sometimes take care of entire functions for a company. It is wise to be informed of this, because what may seem like a core competency of a company which matches your skills, may actually be a function performed by a partner.

- *What is the company's strategy for the next five years?* This includes whether a company is entering new industries or introducing new product lines. Trends such as heavy emphasis on research and development over focusing on a core competency with minimal operating costs can also be valuable information. For example, most auto manufacturers have showcased future cars which utilize alternative forms of energy. It is clear that each of these companies has formed a strategy for growing in what will inevitably become a new market.

- *What are the company's greatest challenges?* If key indicators such as low revenue expectations and a low stock price suggest the company or industry is not fairing well, find out why. Even if a company is profitable, there are always challenges to be faced. For example, many companies are trying to consolidate the various sources of information that flow through financial, production, and customer relationship management systems. Consolidating legacy information systems which use different technology is a great challenge for companies. It is no surprise that Enterprise Asset Integration (EAI) is a growing discipline within information technology that is in high demand.

Specific Criteria

Once you have answers to all your questions regarding a company at a bird's eye view, you may want to drill down to a specific department, location, or group. Here are some questions to help you become well informed regarding your target:

- *What type of work is done within the group?* Try to determine the mission of the group or its responsibilities. A group's function is often centered around a region, industry, product-line, service, or technology.

- *Where within the organization does it fit?* If you can find out under what divisions and leadership a group sits, it can be very impressive to a manager in that area. For example, imagine that after a bit of company research you determine that the Fuel Cell Team is lead by Bill Knudson which is a department under Research & Development and the vice president that leads R&D is Janine Ross.

- *What skills are relevant to the group?* This includes researching what professional disciplines are key to the group's function. For example, a group within a building and construction firm may be composed of civil engineers who specialize in structural engineering and fluid mechanics applied to water flow. This could be key information for a cover letter; if you are not an engineer with those disciplines you could reason that diversifying their workforce to include your area of expertise would bring value to the organization.

- *Is there a growing need for a skill or specialty?* Company organization shifts and changes constantly. Departments are often faced with new challenges which require a different skill set. If you can find out what skills are needed due to a shortage in a specialty, it can be beneficial when marketing yourself.

- *What is the culture like?* This includes what the environment and work/life balance is like for those who work under the group. For example, it may be a sales team that utilizes a "virtual office" environment meaning that electronic communication from home and rotating office schedules take the place of a traditional office setting. Maybe it's a programming group that holds conference calls at 6 AM to "touch base" with the other half of the team in China. Perhaps "Big Grilling Friday" is a tradition where everyone gets off work early for a barbecue. It could be a "work hard play hard" environment where working Saturdays is the norm, but when a deliverable is met, the team takes a few days off to do a social activity. This kind of research can help you find out if a group matches your expectations for a work environment.

After you compile your own custom list of questions to research, you will have realistic goals and measuring the progress of your company research will be simplified. What you research and how much time you spend on it is up to you. The questions listed above are only ideas to get you started. You may want to address a few questions at a time as you progress through searching, applying, and interviewing for a company.

GETTING THE INSIDER VIEW

The best information doesn't come from a news article, earnings report, or company website, but rather from someone with firsthand experience. Someone who has worked for a company, one of its partners, or competitors can give an invaluable perspective that simply cannot be gained by other means.

Example based on a true story

Andrew is a chemical engineering grad student who is looking for a full-time position. He finds out that a small bank specializing in equity research for the pharmaceutical sector prefers to hire candidates with a chemistry background for financial analyst positions. Andrew is able to find a graduate from his university who is an equity analyst and sends her an email with his contact information asking a few questions about life on the job. Sharon is glad to hear from a fellow university alumni and gives Andrew a call. They have a pleasant conversation about her firm and what the daily routine is like. During this conversation Andrew learns what kind of reports financial analysts write on a periodic basis in practice.

Andrew sees an opportunity to differentiate himself from competing candidates and puts aside a few hours to write a similar financial report based on some online examples. After running it by Sharon and making corrections, he sends it in addition to his cover letter for an interview. Andrew is not only called back, but hired for the job in a very short period of time. He later finds out that he was called back, even though they had decided to stop accepting applications, because he was the only one out of five-hundred people to showcase an actual financial report.

Begin by exploring your network—talk to friends, family, co-workers, and professors. A job search may not be a common topic among friends and family; however, try to bring up the subject at least once with everyone in your network. You may be surprised to find out how many industry insiders you are connected to.

Companies often have university ambassadors or representatives who have previously interned for the company they represent. Consult the company career website, your university career center, and/or the public relations office of the company to find out if there is a representative that can answer your company research questions.

Be sure to attend any event which the organization hosts including career presentations and trade shows. In general, company representatives will be happy to share their advice and experience about the organization to help you in your company research. With a bit of charisma and courtesy, you may be offered a business card which will prove useful to get more of your research questions answered.

Once you do find an insider, be sure not to confuse information gathering with interviewing. Your goal is to get your company questions answered, not to market yourself. An insider may avoid contact with you if they are under the impression that you are simply seeking a job. If you are clear in emphasizing that you are researching the company at the current point in time, they may react more positively.

A very effective approach is to contact a company representative and ask to conduct a shadowing or mentoring session. Most company employees are honored to be asked for advice on pursuing their profession. Some universities even have formal shadowing programs or at least are supportive in helping you finding a mentor relevant to your interests.

Keep in mind that it is human nature to enjoy mentoring and giving advice. When afforded a conversation with an insider, be sure they talk most of the time while you steer the conversation with a list of questions. Everyone loves a good listener.

LEVERAGING THE INTERNET

The Internet is unmatched for gathering quick company information. This section provides an overview of where to look for what.

Company Websites

A company's website is almost always the best place to start. It is especially good for high-level criteria and information on the nature of an organization's business. Company career sites are certainly a sound starting point, but other sections are often overlooked such as:

- *Customer information.* Businesses are often far more dedicated to providing information for prospective customers rather than for college candidates. Customer sites are a perfect resource for researching product lines, company locations, business partners, divisions, etc. Additionally, you may find executive briefs, white papers, or case study information targeting customers. For example, see http://www.ge.com/en/product/business.

- *Public relations.* Companies often have public relations sites, usually disguised as "about us" sections, where you can read about their latest advertising campaigns, events, history, and values. You may be able to request printed materials, such as brochures and company newsletters, free of charge, by contacting a company's public relations office or advertising department. See http://www.raytheon.com/about for an example.

- *Investor information.* Corporations nearly always have a section where you can get facts about the company's financial performance including revenue, assets, company size, top management, press releases, company news, and annual reports. For instance, see http://investor.google.com.

General Corporate Research

There are various sites which can help to aggregate company news, strategy plays, and other general information about an industry or organization:

- http://www.bbb.org—*The Better Business Bureau:* Provides company reports on over two million companies.

- http://search.businessweek.com—*BusinessWeek Online:* This search taps into a wealth of world class business related articles.

- http://www.forbes.com/500s, http://www.forbes.com/private500— *Forbes.com:* Offers information on America's five hundred largest companies ranked by sales.

- http://www.fortune.com/fortune—*Fortune Magazine:* Provides a variety of corporate information for investors and job seekers. It is most famous for its information on the top five-hundred companies based on revenue called the "Fortune 500."

- http://www.corporateinformation.com—*Corporate Information:* Includes company and industry research.

- http://answers.google.com/answers—*Google Answers:* Provides customized research for any need at a user defined price. It also has a database of previously asked questions.

Career Research Websites

Sites dedicated to career research, work hard to find corporate information so you don't have to. The following sites provide some examples:

- http://www.vault.com—*Vault:* Provides career resources spanning resume guides, job searches, to researching career paths.

- http://www.wetfeet.com—*WetFeet:* Offers statistics on industries, insider guides, company profiles, and a wealth of other career-related information.

- http://www.careerjournal.com—*Wall Street Journal Career:* A great source for career related articles, news briefs, job hunting, and resume advice.

Financial Information and News

Investment information for corporations can be a significant resource for answering your company research questions. Although not a comprehensive list, here are some ideas:

- http://www.irin.com—*Investor Relations Information Network:* Provides thousands of current and historical annual reports.

- http://pro.edgar-online.com/, http://www.freeedgar.com—*EDGAR Online:* Offers millions of SEC filings for investors.

- http://moneycentral.msn.com/investor—*CNBC Online:* Provides business headlines, key indicator information, and analyst commentary.

- http://finance.yahoo.com—*Yahoo! Finance:* Includes a stock symbol search, a news search, and business articles.

- http://news.google.com—*Google News:* Offers a business section which can prove to be a resourceful search engine for company information.

Online Communities

Company and industry insiders often join online communities such as blogs, forums, news groups, and other community sites. Answering an industry related research question may be as easy as posting a new thread on a forum. Finding a community site greatly depends on the type of company and specific discipline you are targeting. The following sites serve as a small set of examples:

- http://www.eng-tips.com—*ENG-TIPS FORUMS:* Provides forums for nearly every engineering discipline.

- https://www.ieeecommunities.org—*The Institute for Electrical and Electronic Engineers:* This section of the IEEE website provides forums for every area of electrical engineering.

- http://www.mentornet.net—*MentorNet:* A community focusing on mentoring women in engineering and science.

- http://fastlane.gmblogs.com—*General Motors FastLane blog:* Executive blog for General Motors.

- http://www.ibm.com/developerworks/blog—*IBM Developerworks Blogs:* Blogroll for various IBM fellows, experts, and scientists.

- http://www.orkut.com—*Orkut:* A community site that connects people through a network of trusted friends. Orkut has thousands of member groups called "Communities" which include professional communities for nearly any discipline or organization.

HOW YOUR UNIVERSITY CAN HELP

University career centers often have excellent resources for company research. Additionally, your university should be the starting point for growing your network, in effect, drawing you closer to industry insiders.

Career centers often have information specific to its students, the region, and organizations that hire at the respective university. The following list has some examples of what you can find by consulting a university career center:

- Statistics on what organizations hire from your university and major

- Information on research at your university funded by companies

- Contact information for university ambassadors and college HR representatives

- Information on joining alumni lists and groups for a particular major or industry

- Starting salary figures for a specific field regarding graduates from your university

- Free subscriptions or access to career publications such as Vault and WetFeet guides

Some universities even provide career counselors. You may want to go over a list of company research questions with a counselor. The counselor may be able to answer some of your company questions right on the spot or may refer you to a knowledgeable contact.

Companies often hold seminars at universities which can range from resume advice, company overviews, to research talks. They rarely lead to an invitation for an interview, however, you can certainly raise your hand and ask some company questions. Even if you are not interested in working for an organization holding such a session, they may be part of the industry for one of your target companies; for example, a business partner.

RESEARCHING AT PUBLIC OR UNIVERSITY LIBRARIES

The advantage that a library has over the Internet is that it offers publications for free that would otherwise cost a subscription or a purchase. This section describes what information you would be hard pressed to find elsewhere—free of charge.

Most libraries offer access to printed materials such as popular newspapers, magazines, and trade journals. American Demographics, Barron's Magazine, Forbes, and The Wall Street Journal, are some examples—just to name a few.

Trade journals can provide key industry information. Trade journals focus on a specific industry such as "Air Transport World" which is a trade journal for airline managers and "Enterprise Systems Journal" which is for computer scientists managing large systems. Be sure to use the search tools available at the library to find the most relevant printed publications.

Libraries also provide access to enormous research databases, such as FirstSearch and InfoTrac, that would otherwise cost a subscription fee. Your library may even have access to databases targeting businesses such as Business Source Premier and Wilson Business.

Finally, there is no escaping the value of a solid library reference book. Some of the most important facts about organizations can be found in company registry and directory books. Here are some examples:

Standard & Poor's Register of Corporations, Directors and Executives—provides information on top officers, company size, and sales figures.

Hoover's Handbook of American Business, Hoover's Handbook of Private Companies—offer company overviews, history, locations, product information, competitor analysis, and revenue charts.

THE BARE MINIMUM TO DO

As this chapter shows, there can be no end to the information available when doing company research. What is important, is that you know where to find information and that you have a realistic plan to execute. Here is the bare minimum to do assuming you are customizing a resume for an important company or preparing for a career event with a week as your timeline:

1. *Make a list of questions to serve as research criteria (20min).* Be sure to research what services or products the company provides, how it is organized, where its main offices are located, and any recent trends.

2. *Take advantage of any trade or career events hosted by the organization (1 hour).* They can serve as a means to get your research questions answered. For example, the company may host a "virtual event" such as a webcast within the week which is open for questions to the public.

3. *Visit your public library and make use of the Internet (3 hours).* Work through the items on your company research list by consulting freely available trade articles from a public library, online career resources, community forums, investor resources, or any other sources cited in "Leveraging the Internet" and "Researching at public or university libraries."

4. *If possible, find an insider (3+ days).* As discussed in "Getting the insider view," consult any company representatives who cover your university, alumni or students at your university that have worked for the organization, and your network of family and friends.

Profile
Tyron J. Stading

Who do you work for, what is your official job title, and where is the job located?

I'm a Software Engineer for IBM Software Group under Integrated Solutions for the Energy and Utilities sector. I work out of IBM's Austin, Texas campus.

Was it your first choice?

Originally, IBM wasn't even on my radar of companies to work for. IBM's Extreme Blue internship program gave me a different perspective. I realized that a large company can have unmatched resources and entrepreneurial qualities.

However, this didn't stop me from interviewing at a dozen companies including Google, Oracle, HP, Hindspring, VMWare, Network Physics, and Pervasive Software. My goal was to find an environment where I would have the freedom to be involved in the development of enterprise quality software end-to-end. I wanted to gain mastery in the entire development cycle from the generation of a novel idea—to designing the architecture—all the way to the release. I found that opportunity in my current position.

What are some positive aspects of the job?

My team founded a new enterprise product offering. We are working on rapid development framework to connect enterprise systems using business integration adapters. I've had the opportunity to see it grow from an idea to a functional product meeting IBM's product certification. I enjoy the wide array of experiences this type of work entails including brainstorming ideas on a whiteboard, developing a practical framework, working on a code base of my team's design, implementing internationalization of the product, and doing various forms of industrial strength testing such as functional and interoperability testing.

I also have exposure to very senior technical experts on a daily basis and work with exciting emerging technologies.

What are some negative aspects?

When you are building something as large as we are, it can seem to move slow at times. There are so many pieces that need to interlock and steps to follow that a single phase of software development can last months.

I don't think this is necessarily a negative aspect or an issue tied to my position or field, but whenever you start a job you have to prove your quality to everyone new you meet. It takes a lot of work to build credibility so your ideas can receive attention however brilliant they are.

I've found that the software industry is often driven by politics that directly influence the success of products. For example, different organizations and groups have their own measures of performance and their own customers to focus on. Getting heterogeneous intellectual resources working together can be a challenge.

What is your typical day like?

I get in around 8:30 AM and spend the first thirty minutes reading email. About the next hour is spent on doing various forms of research. The work we do has never been done before, so I spend a lot of time reading, talking with experts, and searching for new ideas to approach problems.

By 10 AM or so, I usually start meeting with my team which is composed of two software architects and six engineers. I spend a lot of time at the white board brainstorming ideas. We often discuss software design issues, time lines, validation of ideas, and the integration of various technologies that we use.

Lunch is usually around noon. Unless there is a special event, we normally have lunch at the IBM cafeteria for about thirty minutes. After lunch, I continue meeting with my team and often do conference calls with experts inside and outside of IBM.

I normally spend my time in the late afternoon and evening developing actual code. By this time everything is quiet and peaceful; I find it perfect for software development. My time is normally divided as follows:

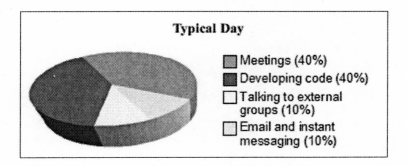

How did you make initial contact with IBM?

I would consider my initial contact to be with IBM Extreme Blue. I applied online with a letter and my resume. The letter included my thoughts on trends in the information technology industry, my interests in combining technical and business skills, and my philosophy on a "work hard play hard" lifestyle.

What type of research did you do on IBM prior to working there?

I researched how strong of a cultural fit it would be for me. I looked at what kind of people work there, what the atmosphere is like, what people say about the culture, and their values. The company's interest in their employees was important for me. I also considered openness to new ideas and how flexible the hours are.

Strategy was a key research topic for me as well. I wanted to make sure that I was passionate about their future strategy and technology. I did organizational research such as who the leading officers of the organization are, who holds the responsibility over different technologies, and how the company is divided into groups. I also looked into their performance compared to their competition in various markets.

Finally, a very important topic in my company research was whether I could make an impact. I wanted to make sure someone like me coming out of college could be an agent of change. I want to look back ten years from now and see that I have fundamentally changed the emerging information age in some way.

What did you learn from all this research?

I found blanketed research of a large organization to be ineffective. The most interesting information I found about the company was when I drilled down to a group with a mission that interested me. I also found that it is often the case that the most hyped technology for a company is not the most profitable. For example, Web Services is one of the most talked about technologies today, but few organizations are making a lot of money from it.

What advice do you have for someone researching an organization?

Make sure you have a clear understanding of the company's vision for the future and position in the market. Try to find out about the people you would be working with in the organization. I personally like to Google people's names. Are they famous externally as well as internally? If you move to a different organization later and the big names you worked with are only known internally within your previous employer, you lose that added recognition.

You have very impressive interviews under your belt. What other advice do you have for candidates?

Try to break out of the preset path for interviews. Everyone's perspective is of great value. If you are waiting in a lobby, chat with a receptionist to get their thoughts and opinions on the organization.

Passion can make up for a lack of knowledge. The night before an interview, I read an entire book on Palm OS programming because it was a new area to me that I found fascinating. It was clear that I was not the most qualified candidate for the position, but I was their first choice because of my excitement and enthusiasm. This is another reason research is important; it can help you find what you are passionate about which in itself creates opportunities.

When learning and building accomplishments, focus on valuable skills rather than a specific product. For example, consider OS/2 an operating system IBM built during the 80's and 90's. The people that focused on the technology in OS/2—such as architecting an enormous software project, its memory management system, and operating system fundamentals—probably have strong careers right now because they emerged from their previous work with marketable skills. Those who focused on skills relevant only to the product—such as technical support or custom OS/2 code libraries—were probably left with less transferable skills after OS/2 was discontinued.

What would you do differently if you could do it all over again?

When I was interviewing, I focused primarily on software development positions. I think when you are interviewing, it is an excellent time to gain a perspective on different career paths. I would have kept an open mind to interviewing for other roles—such as consulting, marketing, and sales positions—to find out what excites professionals in those fields.

Note: At the time of this book's publication, Tyron was no longer a Software Engineer, but rather IBM's Software Architect for the Energy and Utility sector.

TYRON STADING
P O Box 12345
Stanford, CA 94309

Education 1998-Present	**STANFORD UNIVERSITY** Expected Bachelor of Science degree in Computer Science in June 2002. Coursework: OOP, Concurrency, Networking Systems, Distributed Systems, Security, Privacy, File Systems, Resource Recovery/Management, Ad Hoc Networks, Encryption, GUI Design, Compilers, and Databases	**STANFORD,** **CA**
Patents	**Patent Pending** • Dynamic appliance for mobile, flexible, and secure computing • Hardware management component for fail-safe computing • Managed peer-to-peer communications platform for mobile and reliable computing	
Experience January 1999- Present	**PROFESSOR MARY BAKER, MOBILE COMPUTING GROUP** **Research Assistant** • Research and design mobile networking technologies and possible implications, focusing largely on Internet security, peer-to-peer, and privacy issues • Propose and create system designs for the Mobile People Architecture (MPA). which consolidates multiple forms of communication into one dynamic source • Design and implement Palm interfaces with database management for MPA	**STANFORD,** **CA**
June 2001- August 2001	**IBM EXTREME BLUE** **Software Engineer** • Risk Manager is a centralized intrusion detection system that correlates security information • Re-architect Risk Manager for faster throughput, scalability, and extensibility. • Design and develop new products, including an automated attack response system • Responsible for upcoming product release addressing security for server farms	**AUSTIN, TX**
March 2000 - September 2000	**JARNA** **Software Engineer** • Jarna is a platform that synchronizes between wired and wireless devices, leveraging distributed systems • Work under CEO for product design, server architecture, and commercial implementation, specifically authentication, messaging system, file server, and session management • Aid in marketing strategy that leveraged our platform with a peer-to-peer market play	**MENLO** **PARK, CA**
June 1999 - January 2000	**ELECTRONICS FOR IMAGING** **Web Development Engineer** • Responsible for administration and technical aspects of EFI's Internet and Intranet sites • Create tools in Perl/SQL to better facilitate the posting and updating of information by our Marketing, Technical Support, and Human Resource teams. • Consolidate components of programs into libraries and establish standards in site architecture to make better use of existing code and solutions.	**SAN** **MATEO, CA**
June 1997 - August 1998	**TEXAS STATE SENATOR ELIOT SHAPLEIGH** **Intern Director, Legislative Aide** • Conducted original research into government policies for direct implementation • Extensive involvement with computer management and constituent interaction • Responsible for coordinating the work of five interns, including project creation and team management	**EL PASO,** **TEXAS**
Other **Experience** August 2000 – Present	**STRONGBOX NETWORKS** **Co-founder/Inventor** • Invented device that leverages intelligent networks to increase security, mobility, redundancy, and management • Finalist in Stanford E-Challenge (top 5 of 55 teams entered, only undergraduate team)	**STANFORD,** **CA**
Scholarships	**NATIONAL COCA-COLA SCHOLAR** • One of 50 Scholars chosen from 120,000 applicants nationwide • Recognized for accomplishments in academics, leadership, and community service **TOYOTA SCHOLAR** • One of 100 Scholars chosen from all high school students nationwide • Recognized for accomplishments in academics, leadership, and community service	**1998** **1998**
Skills/Software	Industry development work in **C, C++, Java, Python, Perl, XML, Java Script, HTML, HDML, WAP/WML, Zope, and Jabber Instant Messaging** Educational development and knowledge of **UNIX, TCP/IP, Protocols, SSL, Palm, SQL, XML, CGI, Firewalls, Linux, VPN, Embedded Systems, and Lisp**	

5

Secrets of Applying Online

Inevitably, if you seek employment, you will do an online application of some form. Although the information age has found ways to speed up the process of seeking and applying for a job, it is not without trade-offs such as added complexity and a lack of human interaction. You may become cynical or disillusioned with the process considering every company has their own custom submission form, instructions, and rules. You may be thinking there is little hope in competing against the thousands if not millions of other applicants participating. Fear not, because this chapter explains how to sort through the jungle that is the realm of the online job seeker.

The predominant attitude regarding applying online among many candidates is rather ironic, because they are under the assumption that technology has made a job search trivial. They are under the impression that fully utilizing online tools is a quick affair that can be done within minutes. If job leads don't result instantly, they assume applying online doesn't really work or isn't worth the time.

In reality, online tools are far more effective than the best search tools available just a decade ago such as company directories and professional journals. Applying online cannot, however, work miracles. You need to be persistent in using the most effective online tools over time. With a little bit of planning, organization, and the advice in this chapter—you'll put the Internet to work hard for you.

HOW TO GET STARTED

The best way to start is to apply directly on websites for companies and organizations. You may want to consult a company registry or list of employers such as the Fortune500 to generate ideas. *Chapter 4: Researching an Organization* can help in generating your list of target employers.

Industry and Regional Career Sites

There is a wealth of regional, industry, and vocational-specific content to explore. Many newspapers have moved their classified sections online. Check the major papers for surrounding metropolitan areas. The Chicago Tribune's job section found at http://www.chicagotribune.com/classified/jobs is an excellent example.

Your state employment office can be a valuable asset in your online job search. Consider California's employment website found at http://www.spb.ca.gov/employment as an example. Here are some more sources that can help you find regional, industry, and other job postings:

- http://www.rileyguide.com/jobs.html—*The Riley Guide:* Famous for its comprehensive list of resources for job seekers.

- http://www.jobhuntersbible.com/jobs/jobs.php—*Job Hunters Bible:* Website by Richard Bolles, author of the classic career book *What Color is Your Parachute?*

- http://www.quintcareers.com—*Quintessential Careers:* Provides a job search by region and extensive career advice.

Job Banks and Career Services

These websites provide job listings and resume databases that employers often search:

- http://www.collegerecruiter.com

- http://www.careerbuilder.com

- http://www.monster.com

CREATING A TEXT RESUME

Very few online submission forms accept anything other than a text version of your resume. Although it is difficult to make a text resume stand out, and it may not be as visually appealing, the simple format does facilitate easier customizing for each employer. Implementing a customizable resume, as described in *Chapter 2: Crafting a Successful Resume*, is as easy as pasting sections in and out of your text resume.

To get started, save your traditional resume in text format. For example, in Microsoft Word click **File » Save As...**and select **Text Only (*.txt)** from the "Save as type" menu.

The result can be a little discouraging at first. Fonts, colors, and text formatting such a italics are not represented in a plain text document. So, the font that the recipient of your text resume sees is dependent on the program it is opened with. To simplify editing a text resume and to make sure no unsupported formatting is used, it is best to use a plain text editor such as Microsoft Notepad. Notepad can be opened under **Start » All Programs » Accessories » Notepad** under Windows.

There are two plain text document formats—ascii and unicode. You can select which format to save in when using Notepad under **File » Save As...**and by selecting either ANSI (a form of ascii) or UTF-8 (a form of unicode) under the "Encoding :" drop-down menu.

The older of the two formats is the American Standard Code for Information Interchange or ascii (pronounced askee). An ascii document has no formatting other than white space and is restricted to 127 characters. These are essentially the characters available on your keyboard (the remaining characters are not visible such as a carriage return). This format is always guaranteed to work and is the best choice when pasting your resume into an email, because there are still many email programs that accept only ascii plain text.

Unicode, a newer plain text format, is a character set with tens of thousands of visible characters. It is worth creating a unicode resume for its richer characters for website resume submissions. Most of its characters are not very useful for your needs since they are for foreign languages, scientific symbols, etc. In fact, you really only have a few more characters to work with over the ascii set that are relevant to writing a text resume. Figure 5-1 illustrates some characters you may find useful.

Modern web based forms support most unicode characters since the update of the HTML standard in 1997 (to be completely precise, the character set for HTML 4.0 is called the Universal Character Set). See http://www.w3.org/TR/REC-html40/charset.html for more information.

Symbol	Name	Unicode
•	Bullet	2022
‾	Overline	00AF
—	Horizontal line	2500
·	Centered dot	007B
»	Double angle carrot	00BB
²	Square superscript	00B2
½	One-half fraction	00BD

Figure5-1. Some useful unicode characters

Unfortunately, what online forms support varies. What is certain, is that they support Unicode 2.0 which is also referred to the Latin-1 character codes. See http://www.bbsinc.com/symbol.html for a list of these characters. The characters shown in Figure 5-1 have been tested on various career websites for compatibility (including Moster.com).

Just because the HTML form can read in unicode characters, doesn't mean the underlying computer system supports the characters. Read the instructions for the career website carefully for any rules detailing what type of plain text is allowed. If the submission site corresponds to an important employer on your list, you may want to email their webmaster or technical support to make sure. Most career sites have a preview feature or allow you to view your text resume after submission.

A convenient way to find and select unicode characters is to use the Microsoft Character Map utility found under **Start » All Programs » Accessories » System Tools » Character Map** for Windows.

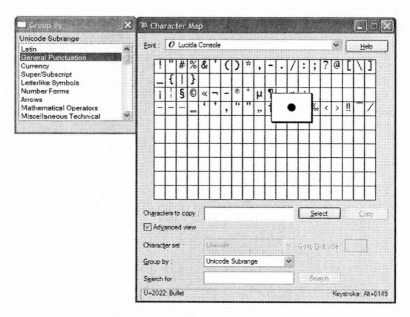

Figure 5-2. Microsoft Character Map

The selection in the "Font :" drop down menu is very important. Most of the fonts include a different set of symbols. We used Lucida Console to find the characters when creating the example text resume at the end of this section. To select a character to paste into your text resume, click **Select** and then **Copy**. If using Notepad, open your text resume and then select **Edit » Paste**.

You can see characters by category by selecting **Advanced view and Unicode Subrange** under the "Group by :" menu. If you want to use the characters in Figure 5-1 be sure the unicode number is the same as the one at the bottom-left corner of the screen; many characters look alike, but have a different code.

An interesting challenge in writing a text resume is alignment. Tabs cannot be relied upon because the tab size can be different when the recipient of the document opens it. Regular spaces are of little use in alignment either because the size of a space depends on the default font type of the text viewer or editor. Figure 5-3 illustrates a text resume that has some problems as we will see shortly.

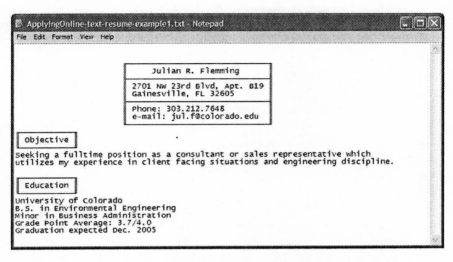

Figure 5-3. Poorly crafted text resume from the view of the author

The default font for the text editor has the same width for each character. This misled the author to use spaces to align his name. The author has made clever use of unicode characters to create borders around headings, but does not realize that the alignment of the border edges rely on the font type.

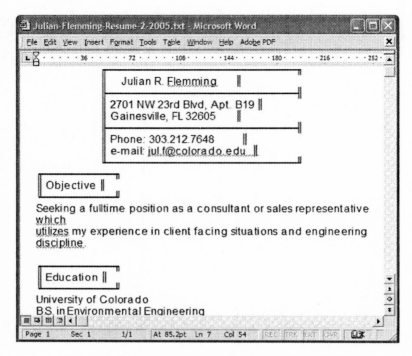

Figure 5-4. Poorly crafted resume from the recipient's view

The problems are evident in Figure 5-4 where a font that does not have identical character spacing is used. A good rule of thumb is to left justify everything in a text resume. Another problem is that the author manually inserted a carriage return after the word "representative" in the objective text. This resulted in the word "which" on its own line. Something else to note is that the unicode characters used for the double line borders, such as those around the objective, are not Unicode 2.0 characters and may not work for many online submission sites.

The width of the reader's viewing area and whether the document will be text wrapped is unknown. Thus, avoid unnecessary carriage returns in text resumes whenever possible even if the text goes past your own viewing area. When you are finished editing your text resume, turn text wrap on and resize the width of the window to a few inches. This helps to catch alignment problems. Text wrap can be enabled in Microsoft Notepad under **Format » Word Wrap**.

Keywords are an essential part of your strategy for applying online. Keywords are a collection of skills, competencies, and industry jargon that are in your text resume for the sole purpose of increasing your resume's visibility during employer candidate searches. A list of words and acronyms separated with single spaces or commas is the standard approach.

There are times when keywords are less appropriate. Your text resume should not always include a keywords section. For example, if you are applying for a specific position, such as "Entry Level Accountant," at a company website use a skills section instead of a keywords section. In this case, it is most important that the resume is tailored for the position rather than for a database search.

Continuing with, Melissa Barnes, the candidate from *Chapter 2: Crafting a Successful Resume,* here is an example unicode text resume created in Microsoft Notepad:

Melissa-Barnes-(C.E.)-UWASH-Jan-8-2006.txt

Melissa Barnes

2701 NW 23rd Blvd, Apt. B91
Seattle, WA 98104
Phone: 206.333.7748
e-mail: mb@washington.edu

Objective

To better secure our country's assets using my knowledge of cryptography and
technology

Education

University of Washington
Seattle, WA
B.S. Computer Engineering May, 2008
Overall GPA 3.2/4.0

Internet Technology Architect

November 2004 - Present
West Park Animal Clinic
http://west-park-url.org
Bellevue, WA

"Melissa has single handedly created new ways for our business to grow" - owner

Designed website using open source technology including:
• Public appointment calendar
• Personal record access
• Knowledge base
• Monthly newsletter from lead veterinarian

Implemented state-of-the-art computer security techniques:
• Advanced Apache configuration
• Router/firewall setup
• Modern web authentication
• Advanced Unix administration

Featured as "Best veterinary website for Seattle" — Oregon Pet Magazine, Jan. 2005

Open Source Enthusiast

July 2003 — present
"Nice work. We've been waiting for that bug fix for a while now." — WebCalendar
mailing list

Open source developer and administrator.
• Familiar with industry leading open source technology

Contributor to:
• WebCalendar PHP online calendar, http://webcalendar.sourceforge.net
• phpMyAdmin data administration tool, http://phpmyadmin.sourceforge.net

Configure and administer:
• MySql database system, http://mysql.org
• Apache web site server, http://apache.org
• FreeBSD unix operating system, http://freebsd.org

Page 1

Melissa-Barnes-(C.E.)-UWASH-Jan-8-2006.txt

Activities

- Seattle SecureWorld Expo, October 2004
- ACM programming competition, September 2004
- Society of Women Engineers (SWE)
- Institute of Electronic and Electrical Engineers (IEEE)

Keywords

Programmer, network security, high availability, cryptography, encryption, reliability, PGP, RSA, PKI, peer-to-peer, P2P, C, C++, Java, perl, javascript, JSP, servlet, XML, Linux, kernel, database, persistence, SQL, CVS

Interests

- Public key cryptography
- Volleyball
- Fencing

TIPS FOR APPLYING BY E-MAIL

During recruitment for an organization it is likely that at some point you will need to send a copy of your resume by email. Here are some tips for applying via email:

- *Take emails as seriously as written letters.* Avoid sending an email as soon as you type it. Save it as a draft or send it to yourself and read it out load word-by-word. Even if the recipient is just an HR assistant, emails are often circulated in the organization at every step of the hiring process.

- *Avoid "chat speak."* Even though "Thx ttyl :-)" may sound cute to you, it is unprofessional.

- *When possible, don't use attachments.* For a variety of reasons, emails with attachments are often ignored. Computer systems may filter out attachments and many organizations have polices where unconfirmed attachments cannot be opened. One advantage of having a text resume is that you can put it in the body of an email. You may also want to consider uploading the fully formatted version of your resume to web space and putting the URL in the email to be downloaded at the recipient's convenience.

- *Create a separate email address for your career search.* This can help you to keep records of your correspondence and protect your privacy. It is important to check this address often because recruiting can happen sporadically. Consider forwarding your career address to your primary email service.

- *Send your cover letter in the body of an email.* A customized cover letter is perfect for an initial email to an employer. Be sure to left justify everything to ensure it looks okay in plain text.

- *Consider sending more than one resume.* If you are not sure which version of your resume to use, feel free to give the recipient the choice. For example, you could say "I have appended both the computer science and sales engineering versions of my resume. The objectives should serve as a guide to selecting which is most appropriate."

- *Use a descriptive name.* Names such as "Resume" are not very helpful to the recipient and can get saved over by documents from other candidates with the same name. Useful information to include in a filename is your name, the date, your major, and your university.

• *Make sure your email program or service is set to use plain text.* Otherwise, your emails may look noticeably different to the recipient. You may want to print your email before sending it to check formatting. So you don't have to hunt through help files, Figure 5-5 shows how to enable plain text for some popular email clients and services.

Program	Version	Menu Navigation
Outlook Express	6.0	Tools » Options... » Send » Mail Sending Format » Plain Text
Eudora	6.2	Tools » Options » Styled Text » Send Plain text only
Gmail	n/a	Toggle between "Rich formatting » " and "« plain text"
Yahoo! Mail	n/a	Mail options » General Preferences » Composing E-mails » Compose messages as plain text
MSN Hotmail	n/a	Compose » Tools » Rich-text editor OFF

Figure 5-5. Plain text email settings

STARTING A WEEKLY ROUTINE

Many internet job seekers become quickly overwhelmed with the landscape of applying online. Don't be the candidate that gives up and just posts his or her resume on Monster.com! The biggest secret of applying online is to take your time. Create a long term plan and execute it periodically as time allows.

The best approach is to keep a list of target employers, resume database sites, and career search sites. Use bookmarks or a simple table to keep direct links to relevant pages such as candidate profiles and open position searches. The advantage of saving the links to search results is you can check the search query again with a click of a button. This way you don't have to re-enter the search parameters such as the industry, occupation, location, etc. Pay close attention to the address bar of the results page. If it is a very long web address with words from your search parameters, then it can be saved and used again as a direct link. Consider scheduling a few hours out of the week to go through your list of links and check for new job postings.

Many sites have "job agents" which automatically email you when a position is open, so you will need to return to these websites less frequently. However, most company career sites do not notify candidates when they post new positions; it can make a huge different if you check back periodically to these sites. Figure 5-6 illustrates an example of a bookmark list for our example candidate, Melissa Barnes.

Notice that she has listed the search parameters she used when creating the direct links to searches under "Description."

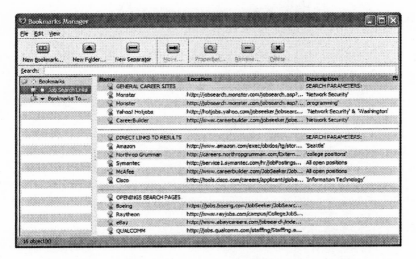

Figure 5-6. Example of career links using browser bookmarks

A spreadsheet or table can work as well—simply copy links from your address bar into the table cells. If you decide to use a table, consider using the following fields:

- *Description:* The company's name and the type of link(s).

- *Link(s):* Website URLs.

- *Cover letter:* Filename of the cover letter submitted if applicable.

- *Resume:* Filename of the resume submitted if applicable.

- *Agent:* Whether you were able to sign up for an agent notification service.

- *Date:* The date so you know when you last visited.

If you use descriptive naming for your cover letter and resume filenames, you will always know what version of your documents each employer has. Of course, you can also use a combination of bookmarks and some simple records to achieve the same results as a spreadsheet. Consider taking an hour once a week to go through some of your links and record your progress.

STRATEGIES FOR GAINING AN EDGE

If you're still not convinced that you can stand out from other online job seekers, consider some of these tips:

- *Follow the directions.* Pace yourself and make a point to look at the instructions or frequently asked questions page before applying at a company website. If you had hundreds of people emailing you everyday wouldn't you be annoyed when someone doesn't give you the information you need in the right format for the thousandth time?

- *Put a title or quote at the beginning of your submission.* In many cases, the 15 minute rule (as suggested in *Chapter 2: Crafting a Successful Resume*) is more like a 2 second rule for online applications. Having something at the top to get their attention can make the difference. For example, "Pharmacist with two years of hospital experience" could serve a candidate well.

- *Reposition the content of your resume.* Match your skills to the needs of the position and put the most relevant content at the beginning. *Chapter 4: Researching an Organization* can help you in finding ways to match your skills.

- *Always check if a job agent is available.* Job search and application sites often have agents that send an email when a new position is listed that matches your profile.

- *Re-post your submission often.* When employers search for eligible candidates, the candidates that have posted their profiles recently often are at the top. If you resubmit your profile, you may be able to bump yourself up the list.

- *Utilize multiple profiles.* You may want to consider customizing your profile for different locations or departments of an organization.

- *Check your submission after a few days.* Not all online forms were created equal. Sometimes profiles are only partially submitted or some other errors occur. Additionally, having another look can catch mistakes.

- *Ignore salary fields.* Whenever possible, leave "desired salary" and "previous salary" fields blank. See *Chapter 10: Understanding Human Resources—HR interviews, salary negotiation, & more* for information on negotiating salary.

- *Type essay questions in a word processor.* Just because it is an online form doesn't mean bad grammar and "chat speak" can be excused. Open up your favorite word processor and proofread it like a traditional essay.

THE BARE MINIMUM TO DO

You could spend everyday hunting for a job online (and many unemployed people do). Here is the bare minimum to do assuming it is the beginning of your last semester in college:

1. *Create an ascii text version of your resume and cover letter with descriptive filenames.*

2. *Make a separate plain text file to customize your resume.* This file should contain extra content to paste in and out of your text resume such as different objectives, projects, credentials, work experience, leadership experience, etc.

3. *Compile a list of 20+ websites.* The list should include target employers, general career websites, regional sites, and industry-related sites. You may want to look at a company registry or ranking as described in *Chapter 4: Researching an Organization* as well.

4. *As time allows, submit a cover letter and resume to each website on your list.* Bookmark any links to job opening search pages along the way.

5. *Create a long-term plan for applying to open job postings from the list.* Build bookmarks to reflect your plan.

6. *Schedule a half-hour once or twice a week to execute your plan.*

Profile
David Winkler

Who do you work for, what is your official job title, and where is the job located?

I work for Intel Corporation as a Design Engineer. I work on CPU development for the Desktop Platform Group in Portland, Oregon.

Was it your number one choice?

Yes—it is definitely my dream job. If someone during college had told me I could become a design engineer for a premier Intel processor, I would have said "No way. I'm not qualified enough. I don't have a Ph.D. and I'm not a super genius." The next best offer I had was for the defense industry, which actually paid more, but the work was not as interesting and I didn't like my primary interviewer—he was arrogant. The location was not very exciting compared to Portland either.

What are some positive aspects of your current position?

I love my job. I grew up around computers—I remember tinkering around with a Macintosh 2GS when I was ten and I clearly remember the day my family got a Pentium 100 at the beginning of high school. Computer Engineering was a natural choice for me and this job is exactly in line with why I got into my field in the first place.

Something that is important to me is how much of an impact my job has. So many people use the product that I work on for everyday use and business. Even scientists using supercomputers are affected by my work. I remember during my first days of work, my boss was explaining a learning assignment to me and said "We have some circuits here dangling that aren't really used, if you could write a perl script to get rid of those you could save a milliwatt of electricity. That may not seem like much to you, but multiply that by millions of users over decades of use and you are making quite a difference in the world's energy consumption." We both joked about it, but there certainly is some truth to that statement.

My superiors constantly emphasize that I own my career. That freedom really makes a difference for me, because if I wanted to move to tech marketing next year, for example, everyone would be supportive. Management does a lot of one-on-one sessions with me with great down to earth advice explaining things like how I can look good compared to my peers and what expectations I should have of my job.

I work in an open office environment where everyone is equal. I work near a vice president who has the exact same desk and setup as me. It promotes communication—I feel that I can go talk to anyone when I am curious about something.

The management I work with does an amazing job of communicating no matter what level they are at. They are very open to explaining exactly why decisions are made. If I don't have time to watch the talks in person, I often watch online and have the opportunity to submit live questions.

What are some negative aspects?

As I mentioned before, I love my job. Just like any work environment, mine is not perfect. People often find the technical nature of my position negative. This is not really a negative for me since it's what I really wanted to do. I've always been interested in technical things, for example, I took apart my Xbox recently. It's a deep technical job and specific technical skills are what I'm maturing rather then management, client facing, or presentation skills. After a few years I'll probably start to look at gaining other types of skills, but for now I'm happy.

What is your typical day like?

I get in at 8 AM. This is totally optional, we have the freedom to work our hours however we want. I like to get there earlier because I get more work done in the morning and I think it looks good if I'm already at my desk before management arrives.

My next step is just to get settled. I catch up with my e-mail, look at my calendar, and check the status of simulations run overnight. The rest of my day consists of designing circuitry, running simulations, talking to experts when I have questions, and going to meetings. So my time consists of:

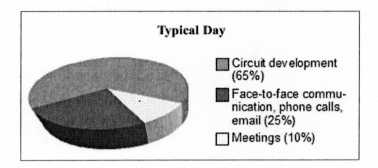

How did you make initial contact with Intel?

My initial contact was at a University of Florida career fair. I told the recruiter that I was interested in a rotational program. They seemed interested during the career fair, but they never got back to me. I then spent a great deal of time tailoring my resume toward my goal—circuit design. I expanded out the projects I had worked on and emphasized why I would make a knowledgeable circuit design engineer. I took a lot of graduate coursework related to circuit design which really helped. I then applied online at the Intel website.

After a few weeks I was sent a survey by e-mail asking me what I was interested in, what locations for Intel I would prefer, my GPA, and graduation date. They were interested in manufacturing—I told them I have an interest in circuit design, however emphasized that working for Intel would be great in manufacturing too.

Then I received a phone call out of the blue for my first interview—on the spot.

What was your first interview like?

It was on the phone without any preparation. My interviewer asked if that would be alright. I quickly decided that having it on the spot would be best because I didn't want to lose the opportunity to scheduling problems or to other candidates. I'm the type of person which likes to prepare and take my time for things, so I was very nervous.

It lasted about an hour and was 75% technical and 25% behavioral.

The first question was to solve a Boolean equation. The trick was that the OR operation is distributed. I didn't remember this which many freshman electrical engineers know quite well—I failed the question. At this point, I thought I was done. I thought to myself "If I can't solve this simply problem how can I possibly ever work for Intel." This is just what I was thinking though, I was very good at keeping my cool during our conversation.

Next were some questions on digital integrated circuit design. I was taking a graduate class in this, so I think I impressed him with my solutions. He also gave me a static CMOS circuit and asked me how to optimize the inputs for speed which I answered successfully.

Then he asked me what questions I had for him. I managed to tell him that I was very interested in what he did. As soon as I said that, he was very happy to tell me about what he was working on and we had an engaging conversation from that point.

What did you think after the phone interview?

Well, the interviewer was very supportive. He said "we have limited availability, but I'm going to recommend you for a site interview." He even told me what to study for the site interview! I spent spring break studying the materials he suggest for the interview and I ended up being well prepared for the upcoming technical interviews.

What were your site interviews like?

I had four site interviews and lunch with my hiring manager. They all started with an intense technical discussion followed by a few casual questions regarding my personality. It was clear that their goal was to push me to the limits of my technical ability—I finished each interview stumped. Each interview covered a different fundamental area of chip design. I remember walking away from the interviews thinking they were the hardest I had ever had. I was certain they would not extend an offer. I even called my parents and told them I didn't make it.

Have any memorable questions?

I remember getting stumped on a circuit layout technique called folding. A behavioral question asking how I cope with a teammate that is troublesome comes to mind a well. They also asked about my internship experience with NASA. They reacted very positively to the fact that I had no job definition and had to work on something that I knew little about, but was successful in the end.

It showed that I was good at finding an expert when I needed help and I take initiative. Now that I work there, I realize that I was really striking a cord with them. I have to talk to experts everyday in order to get my work done.

I was also asked about a difficult decision I had made in the past. I told him that I was a swimmer in college and after a few years, I had to make the decision whether to focus on engineering or continue swimming. We had a very interesting conversation over it, because he too had been a college athlete as a basketball player.

Did you negotiate your compensation package?

No (Intel doesn't negotiate with recent college grads). It was a quick decision for me. They were extremely efficient at getting the offer on the table. I got back from my site interview on Tuesday and got the offer in the mail on Friday. I had a week to decide—it wasn't much of a decision.

What did college prepare you for when it came to landing the job?

My grad school classes were pivotal. My circuit design classes really paid off. Even a week before the interviews, I was learning things that were beneficial.

The career resource center at my university was helpful in giving me some things to think about for my resume. They also were great at explaining how to search for a job and at explaining what to expect. They helped me research what the average salary is for my field and gathering information about employers I was considering.

What were you unprepared for and how would you recommend someone build competency in it?

I wish I had known what I wanted to do. I wish I had honed in on something like VLSI, gained course experience, and gained internship experience in it. I was lucky enough to realize two semesters from graduation that I wanted to do device level circuit design.

David J. Winkler

Email: dwinkler@ufl.edu

Current Address:
112 NW 19th St Apt A
Gainesville, FL 32603
Cell: (352) 514-2983

Permanent Address:
6612 Syfert Ct
Orlando, FL 32818

OBJECTIVE:
To obtain a challenging full-time position at Intel in either Integrated Circuit Manufacturing or Engineering.

EDUCATION:
Masters of Engineering in Electrical Engineering, University of Florida, Expected May 2004 GPA: 3.68
Bachelors of Science in Computer Engineering, University of Florida, May 2003, GPA: 3.86
Graduate Concentration Areas: VLSI, Digital Signal Processing, Analog Circuits

WORK EXPERIENCE:
Graduate Teaching Assistant   *UF Department of Electrical Engineering* Gainesville, FL   Aug. 2003 – Present
- Assisted students and reviewed papers for two graduate courses in digital signal processing.

Systems Engineering Intern   *Jet Propulsion Lab*   Pasadena, CA   June 2003 - Aug. 2003
- Designed Mars mission concept as a part of a 12 member team and helped decide on the mission architecture and science instrumentation necessary to meet science objectives.
- Researched and designed telecommunications subsystem for a constellation of 3 microsatellites orbiting Mars.
- Worked regularly with experienced JPL Engineers in a concurrent design environment to estimate mass, volume, and costs for proposed design and to ensure that the telecommunication subsystem met mission requirements.
- Presented results of concept study to Mars Program Office and drafted a final concept study report.

Research Assistant   *UF Electronics and Communications Lab*   Gainesville, FL   Jan 2002 – June 2003
- Designed radiation tolerant digital circuitry for a wireless communications system for the Department of Energy at Argonne West National Labs.
- Designed and manufactured PCBs using Multisim and Protel CAD tools and programmed a user interface in Labview.
- Designed radiation tolerant Analog to Digital converter from off the shelf parts to be used for data acquisition in the wireless communications system.
- Converted communications system to a microcontroller design using an Atmel ATMega323 microcontroller.

Assistant Network Administrator   *UF International Center*   Gainesville, FL   July 2001- Jan 2002
- Provided technical support to staff and maintained the network including installing network software and upgrading hardware on workstations.

SKILLS/OTHER EXPERIENCE:
Projects:
SRAM IC – Simulated and designed SRAM IC in Cadence including basic storage cells, address decoder, control logic, and sense amps as a part of 4 person team
Analog 1-D Motion Sensor – Simulated and designed complete sub-threshold CMOS analog IC that detects motion in 1 dimension using array of photodetectors
Autonomous Robot – Designed voice activated waiter robot that serves humans
Small 8 Computer – 8 instruction computer designed in VHDL
RF/Fiber Remote – Designed a handheld unit for UF lightning lab researchers capable of testing and acquiring data from remote sensors via RF or fiber optic link
Computer Skills/Languages: UNIX, C, VHDL, Assembly, Java, C++, Pascal, Perl, Basic
Software: Cadence (Composer, Virtuoso, Spectre), Protel, Matlab, Labview, Multisim, PSpice, Sybase, Mathcad

ACTIVITIES:
UF Student Investment Club	August 2003-Present
Tau Beta Pi webmaster	April 2001-Dec. 2001
University of Florida Men's Division I Varsity Swimming Team	Aug. 1999-May 2000
Institute of Electrical and Electronic Engineers	May 2000-Present
University of Florida Chess Club (Rated a chess expert by USCF)	Aug. 1999-Present

HONORS:
Tau Beta Pi , SEC All Academic, Disney Scholar, Golden Key National Honor Society, Edgewater High School Class of '99 Salutatorian, All-State Swimming, WFTV Channel 9 Supergrad, Dean's List, ECE Department Fellowship

6

Mastering Career Fairs

Career fairs are common place for colleges, industries, and regions. They provide an outlet for both employers and candidates to market themselves.

This chapter covers the essentials for marketing yourself successfully to an employer during a career fair. This guide not only applies to traditional university career fairs, but also to regional events, industry fairs, and internal career events such as networking sessions for co-op and intern placement.

WHY CAREER FAIRS ARE WORTH IT

Anyone who has been to a college career fair has experienced the common employer response of "Here's our company card. Please apply online." Being competent enough to find the websites of employers without the help of a fair, you may wonder what advantage attending career fairs can give you. This section explains how career fairs have their place as a step in every job seeker's strategy.

A career fair is an opportunity to have a one-on-one discussion with a representative of an organization. It allows someone to see a hard copy of your resume, rather than an electronic copy from a database. A strong resume tailored to an organization's current business challenges coupled with a good handshake, confidence, charisma, and an engaging conversation can drive a representative to move mountains on your behalf even if the company is not currently hiring.

Career fairs are an excellent source of first-hand information about a target company. You may want to ask a representative why they made the decision to work for the organization. A representative may also provide an email address or business card effectively giving you access to an industry insider for company research.

If it is a company that is high on your list of preferred employers, this contact may prove invaluable in conducting company research as described in *Chapter 4: Researching an Organization*. After meeting your research criteria and goals, the gathered knowledge should prove useful in writing an unmatched cover letter and resume when formally applying for a position. Although a good resource for company information, be sure not to engage employers without at least some background information.

Attending career fairs can also provide a good indicator of which companies are hiring. At one extreme you may see an intern handing out company cards and at the other, a booth filled with representatives covering a diverse array of positions. Additionally, representatives are usually quite honest if you ask them how strong the present demand is for your discipline within their organization.

Finally, it is important to keep the employer's perspective in mind when managing your expectations for career events. Think for a moment as to why employers are so eager to attend career fairs. They certainly may be there to fill immediate positions; however, companies are more likely to attend in order to generate interest around their organization. Unfortunately, hiring happens quite sporadically in most organizations and does not normally center around college graduation dates. Hiring is often done within days of a headcount becoming available—leaving little time for career events.

From the perspective of the hiring manager, a perfect human resources department has the ability to provide a list of exceptional candidates on-demand as soon as he or she needs to hire someone. Thus, HR departments are motivated to get as many resumes into their databases as possible. This is why company representatives at career fairs often seem interested even if no position is available matching your credentials. They often want to get as many strong candidates excited about the organization as possible to increase the available pool for future hiring.

WHERE TO FIND CAREER FAIRS

Ask to see if there is a career service program at your university. They are often set up where the system automatically sends you an announcement about upcoming events or an open position that would suit your profile. Also, individual departments often have lunch-ins and private fairs.

To find out about regional career fairs, call or visit the website of your state employment office. As an example, the employment website for Illinois is http://www.ides.state.il.us/ which has a "Job Fairs and Special Events" section.

There are also online resource dedicated to listing career events. Here are some examples:

- http://www.careerfairs.com—*CareerFairs.com:* Provides a free database search of career fairs categorized by month and profession.

- http://www.nationalcareerfairs.com—*National Career Fairs:* Offers a calendar of fairs and open houses from around the country.

- http://www.jobweb.com/employ/fairs/public_fairs.asp—*JobWeb.com:* Provides a search for college career fairs.

Student organizations often hold career events or provide free access to regional and national career fairs. Check with local chapters at your university. Here are some organizations to serve as examples:

http://www.acm.org—*Association for Computing Machinery (ACM)*
http://www.shpe.org—*Society of Hispanic professional engineers (SHPE)*
http://www.ieee.org—*Institute of Electrical and Electronic Engineers (IEEE)*

FORMING A STRATEGY

Forming a plan and properly preparing for a career fair can ensure everything goes smoothly and gives you added confidence. Start by obtaining a list of the companies attending—preferably with a floor plan and booth locations. Make a list targeting the employers you are most interested in. If necessary, try to narrow down the list until you have one employer for fifteen minutes of your time.

After narrowing down the list, rank the employers. You may also want to pay special attention to your top picks when forming a plan. Tailoring a resume specifically for an organization is certainly worth your time. It is often a good idea to visit key companies at the beginning or end of the event since the representatives may better remember you. If a company high on your list has more than one representative at the career fair, don't hesitate to plan a visit to more than one person representing the same organization throughout the event.

It is often beneficial to attend as early as possible. You may be afforded a longer conversation with your top picks. Another viable strategy is to visit employers you are less interested in first. This can give you a warm up and some confidence before approaching organization you are considering more seriously.

If you want to impress an interested employer, you should consider preparing a portfolio as discussed in *Chapter 7: Learning the Art of Interviewing*. Considering time constraints, you won't be afforded the chance to showcase your portfolio's contents as much as during an interview, but vivid visual examples can be impressive and memorable.

Preparing your attire is also a significant consideration. This greatly depends on the career event. For example, MIT is known for having career fairs where no one wears a suit. On the other hand, you would stick out like a soar thumb if you didn't dress in formal wear at the University of Florida's career showcase. In general, pick something you feel professional and confident in; when in doubt, err on the side of formality. On the other hand, if you are the adventurous type, don't feel you need to be boxed in by rules. For example, it is not uncommon to see "hot shot" programmers attend career events with jeans and a polo shirt of their favorite development tool—they are taken very seriously.

MASTERING YOUR CAREER FAIR PITCH

Having a pitch prepared before a career fair can make quite a difference. Having practiced it before hand, you will be able to communicate key information more efficiently and effectively. Additionally, the added practice can help you to get comfortable in marketing yourself, which for most people is not a very natural topic of conversation. A well rehearsed pitch makes you sound like a confident natural communicator compared to competing candidates.

If you decide to brainstorm a pitch, the next consideration is what content it should include. Here are some guidelines:

1. Begin with your name, degree program, and graduation date

2. Define whether you are seeking a full-time, co-op, or internship position

3. Show your interest for the organization or a particular position

4. Highlight your key credentials

5. Discuss next steps

Career Pitch Example

I'm Kevin. [Firm handshake]
It's a pleasure to meet you Jane.

I'm an Aerospace Engineer with an expected graduation date of May this year. I'm interested in interviewing for a full-time position.

Lockheed is an employer I admire and have followed for years—I was sure to visit your table first. I'm especially interested in research and development of new aircraft.

If you don't mind, I'd like to briefly highlight some of my credentials:

• My GPA is 3.4

- I have research that could bring great value to your organization. I work on ways to improve the success rate of aerospace prototypes.

- I have industry experience. I had an exciting summer internship with Raytheon.

- I have strong leadership skills. I've lead several winning teams in Aerospace competitions.

What are the next steps in the process?

Thank you for your time Jane. [Smile]

As the above example emphasizes, always begin with a good handshake. Although preparing a pitch can pay off when you are talking to a representative that has a very passive conversation style, you need to be flexible in delivering your pitch. Just because the conversation isn't going according to the plan, doesn't mean you should talk out of turn. Representatives will often ask you for the majority of the information in your prepared pitch.

The pitch is most useful in helping you to keep track of whether key information has been covered during a discussion with an employer. For example, toward the end of your time, you may notice that you haven't highlighted why you would be a strong match for the organization. You could finish by saying "One last thing—I'd like to point out a few things on my resume which I think are in line with Apple's needs."

Being polite can go a long way during career fairs. Most career fair representatives arrive late the night before and have been standing for hours talking to student after student. The warmer you are and the easier you make the discussion for them, the more favorably they will look upon you. A common mistake is to hand them a resume before even beginning the discussion. A smart candidate gives a pleasant introduction and doesn't make them read! A few confident remarks on your credentials can be far more effective. You can ask them at the end of the discussion if they'd like to keep a copy of your resume.

If the conversation goes well, ask for a business card. This will allow you to send an immediate thank you email and a follow-up note after a few weeks. Refer to *Chapter 7: Learning the Art of Interviewing* for example thank you notes.

Common Mistakes

1. *Not planning ahead.* Without planning ahead you can end up in embarrassing discussions with representatives and missed opportunities to talk to key employers. A common mistake is to try and talk to every employer at the fair regardless of their relevance. This usually results in awkward discussions with employers that are not interested in your field. You are also likely to lose opportunities to talk with employers that are hiring for your discipline because there simply isn't enough time to visit everyone.

2. *Asking a representative personal questions.* Conversation regarding race, religion, your personal life, or the representative's personal life should be avoided.

3. *Monopolizing a representative's time.* If there is a long line behind you, try to keep your discussion short unless the representative continues to ask you questions. If you find yourself spending more than three minutes delivering your pitch, it is too long.

4. *Not bringing enough resumes.* Bring three resumes for each employer you plan to visit. You may interact with more than one representative at an employer's table. Also, you may be introduced to employers you had not previously considered or employers may attend that were not listed ahead of time.

5. *Refusing to disclose your GPA.* It is acceptable to leave out your GPA from your resume; however, refusing to disclose it when asked by a representative can take you out of the running entirely.

6. *Entering the representative's personal space.* Be sure to keep the appropriate distance from the recruiter. Also, do not stand so far apart such that others can walk between the two of you and interrupt the conversation.

7. *Not following up.* Whenever possible, follow up—it can only give you an advantage over those who don't bother.

8. *Forgetting names of representatives.* Compiling a list of the representatives you meet is essential. You may want to consider bringing a notepad to career events in order to jot down names after each conversation. They can come in handy when addressing cover letters and writing thank you notes. Usually

you can get their email address to follow up with from a recruiter which covers your university or region as well.

Profile
Sandie Cheung

Who do you work for, what is your official co-op title, and where is it located?

I work for The Boeing Company as a Liaison Co-op Engineer at their military facility in St. Louis, Missouri. In the the last year and a half I've had the opportunity to work in several departments: Materials & Processing, TACAIR Materials, Standards and Producibility, Factory Support, and Phantom Works-Metallics Teams. Something else to note is that I recently switched my major to Material Science Engineering from Electrical Engineering.

Was it your first choice?

Yes, since it was my only offer the first year that I attended my university's job fair. I felt that Boeing had many opportunities that I could explore to fit my skills and abilities.

For the summer of 2005 I was offered three internships through the university career fair—Alcoa, Rockwell Collins, and Lockheed Martin Aerospace Company. It was a very difficult decision, but I decided to go back to Boeing for the prestigious internal career fair they offer for potential full-time hire placement. If Boeing did not have the internal career fair I would have loved to go to any of the other three companies to receive more industrial experience. Overall, I think all these companies would provide a lot of insight on advanced metal processing.

What are some positive aspects of the co-op?

My supervisor is very open to letting me explore all the different departments, pertaining to my interest, at Boeing. I often work with chemical, mechanical, and liaison engineers.

A lot of the projects I work on are totally dependent upon me. I have the freedom to plan and execute the problems that are given to me on my own with complete creative freedom.

I've worked on: replacing the adhesive for low energy gum rubber used in the self sealing fuel lines, water soluble lubricant for bending operations of Al and Ti, and insulating foam to a more up to date material. I also study premature fracturing of Hi-Lock collars installed on the skin, advance friction welding for preformed parts, and corrosion resistance of aerospace aluminum alloys. The rest of my time is used to work on process specifications used to build or layup parts; my job is to find and propose more efficient methods.

What are some negative aspects?

At first, I didn't get outside of the lab very often. Recently, through curiously, I've been given permission to spend the majority of my time outside of the lab. I go out to the shop floor to talk to the people assembling and really testing the planes. If I had not taken my own initiative, I wouldn't have seen the planes being assembled and the big picture. The shop floor workers also provide amazing input that helps me with lab testing and generating new ideas.

What is your typical day like?

I go to work at around 7 AM. The first thing I do is write up a little summary of my progress for my supervisor. This usually includes some calculations, conclusions, figures, or graphs. After that I check my email and come up with a plan for what to do for the rest of the day.

At this point I usually go out to the shop floor and talk to the production workers. Sometimes I visit the materials lab or chemical lab first and talk to the technicians there. I usually go to the chemical lab to get updates on my test specimens. If I'm luck, I get some results back.

I usually have lunch with the shop floor workers. I can hear the bell that signals lunch from quite a ways away. It's a great social environment. I think I've found out more about the inner workings of the aerospace industry at lunch than anywhere else.

After lunch, I prepare more samples at the lab, plot data or write a spreadsheet, and sometimes it's time to present my findings to my superiors. It is pretty common for me to stay until 6-7 PM considering that I enjoy my job very much. I like to tidy things up at the end of the day as well. I do a lot of talking too, so I have to make up for it. My day usually pans out like this:

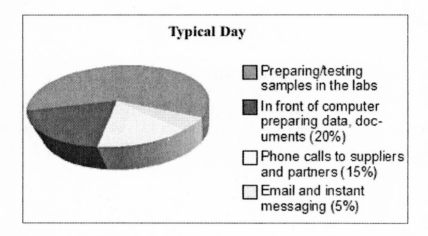

How did you make initial contact with Boeing?

This is my third internship with Boeing. My first contact with them was through a university career fair with about 25 companies. I was a sophomore at the time and attended even though it was primarily filled with juniors and seniors. I talked to all the companies there, but Boeing sounded more interested from my research. It had a co-op program that would allow me to apply my skills.

Coming from a small school, SIUC, I felt like all the companies there were all a great fit for my background. I was willing to work for any of them—just to gain valuable experience.

I think my extensive research background really made me stand out amongst the crowd of engineers. I was able to present my interest in technology through past lab projects and my experiences with colleagues. Because of this, I was able to talk to them extensively compared to the time they spent with most of the other candidates. I think the extra bit of time allowed me to relax and be myself. They called me the day after for an interview.

How did you prepare for your interview?

I did a mock interview with a college professor I've known since high school. The practice really made a difference—I had never done an interview before. I also reviewed my resume extensively making sure I could expand favorably on any point.

Although I didn't take the initiative, I think doing a mock interview with someone you do not know—like a random professor—can be effective since you don't have the luxury of knowing your interviewer ahead of time. Also, get LOTS of sleep—it'll help with nervousness.

What was your interview like?

The interview for my co-op was done on campus at SIUC in the career services building. The interviewer was very nice and outgoing. I felt this eased a lot of my nervousness making it easier to express myself. She asked me a mix of behavioral, HR, and technical questions. She stressed a lot on my leadership, school involvements, and my research projects in the university's chemistry department.

Have any memorable questions?

I was asked how I could contribute to the company. I said that I have a very relevant skill-set and I'm determined to use what I've learned. I explained that I have unique skills to contribute to current research projects and could help accomplish research goals faster. I also mentioned that I was interested in advanced alloys and processing techniques. Finally, I emphasized that I can help Boeing gain an edge over its competitors.

The most interesting interview question I've ever been asked was actually from a Navy engineer. I was presented with an old metal rod. I then was asked what type of metal it was, what type of corrosion had taken place, and at what rate. I was able to guess what type of metal it was, but I had trouble determining that it was efoliating corrosion at an accelerated pace.

How do you prepare for career fairs?

I go through all the attending organizations, make a list to target, and research what the needs of those organizations are at that time. A week before, I go to every workshop my university offers. I have yet to attend a workshop that I didn't learn something from. Some examples are resume writing, career fair prep, and interviewing workshops.

Many of these workshops are put on by the companies themselves. For example, I've attended workshops by Honda and Proctor and Gamble. The supervisor and presenter for Honda actually said "this is exactly what we are looking for," "do not do this," etc. These things make a difference—the University of Illinois is a very competitive school. If you screw up, there is another student in line.

What advice do you have for someone who wants to be successful at a career fair?

Make a plan of the companies you want to go to first and know the table layout. Also, representatives often switch off after lunch or periodically. Sometimes it's best to come back and talk to someone else.

Lookup all the organizations, research them, and find out what they are offering. Plan for what you want to say to each company. Keep in mind that you will have five minutes. Practice talking about the strongest points about yourself. Go over (and over and over) your resume—know it well. Be sure to dress professionally as well. A suit is not necessary, but be sure you are presentable.

SANDIE H. CHEUNG
shcheung@uiuc.edu

Home:	Currently:
1228 Tanglewood Dr.	709 Green St. Apt B13
Herrin, IL 62948	Urbana, IL 61801
(618) 942-6778	(314) 369-3708

Objective   To gain diverse industrial experience in Material Science Engineering through a 2005 summer internship.

Education

August 2000-2002   Southern Illinois University Carbondale
Undergraduate   **Overall GPA: 3.774/4.00**
    Major: Electrical Engineering
August 2003-Present   University of Illinois Urbana-Champaign - Transfer
Undergraduate   **Overall GPA: 3.301/4.00   Graduation : May 2006**
    Major: Material Science Engineering   - Specializing in Metals
    Minor: Matse Business and Mathematics

Experience

Fall 2004-Present   Dr. Jian Ku Shang's Metallics Lab - UIUC
Undergraduate Research
    Studied the use of TiO in eliminating organic materials in water.

Summer 2004   Bauman Technical State University -- Moscow, Russia
Study Abroad Fellowship
    Completed 120 hours of Russian language.
    Explored the Russian aspects on materials research.

Summer 2003   Phantom Works Metallics Team -- Boeing Company
Co-op Student
    Studied the cost efficiency of friction stir welding, hydropillar processing, and linear friction processing in
    perform build-up.

Spring 2003   TACAIR Materials, Producibility, and Standards -- Boeing Company
Co-op Student
    Quantified Cytec Resin and Prepreg by historical data analysis.
    Determined a semi-synthetic, water soluble lubricant suitable for serve Ti and Al bending operations.
    Investigated root cause to Hi-Lock collar failure during installation.

Summer 2002   Analytical Department -- Schering Plough Pharmaceuticals
Internship
    Tested degradation products and pseudo drugs in Clarinex D-12 by HPLC technique.

Spring 2002   Materials and Processes -- Boeing Company
Co-op Student/ Boeing Ambassador
    Analyzed Al alloys for fatigue, fracture, corrosion resistance, tensile, and load.
    Measured corrosion pitting and also Rockwell A hardness in friction stir welded Al-7050.
    Tested adhesion coatings for bare Al alloys.

Summer 1999-2002   Department of Chemistry & Biochemistry - SIUC
Sol-Gel Researcher
    Developed a new practical application for removal of toxic metal ions in water.
    Optimized the luminescence technique in a glucose sensor.
    Worked on developing gold nanoclusters through an internal, matrix, redox potential for quantum dots.
    Worked with the Atomic Emission Spectroscopy (AES), Igor Pro, UV-vis Instrument, and TEM.

Research

Research Experience
    Worked with silica sol-gel precursors (enTMOS, SHTMOS, and TMOS) to develop practical applications and to
    modify existing material applications.
Publication
    Co-author of "Metal-Binding Glasses: Efficient in Removal of Toxic Metal Ions in Water" under preparation for
    the journal *Inorganic Chemistry*.
    Patent pending on "Metal Binding Glasses."
Research Grants
    2001 Chancellor's Research Creative/Activity Award ($1500) -- SIUC
    Summer Apprenticeship Program by MedPrep ($1000) -- SIUC
    American Ceramic Society Travel Award ($300) -ACerS
    International Undergraduate Materials Research Society Award ($1500)- MRS
Conferences
    Poster Presentation -- American Chemical Society, (ACS) Chicago Meeting
    Poster Presentation -- Materials Research Society, San Francisco Meeting
    Poster Presentation -- Inorganic Day, UMSL

7

Learning the Art of Interviewing

After years of battling bell curves, enduring long nights, and manipulating equations until your face is blue, your fate is determined by something entirely unrelated—an hour long conversation which can often be the most awkward, unnatural trial of a career. The fact is, to properly prepare for such an experience you need to learn completely new skills to be successful.

There is no standard written exam or set of criteria that can determine which candidate can bring the most value to an organization. As much as organizations would like to formalize the process, we are complex living, breathing human beings. Organizations invariably select a representative to talk with you and make a decision which they argue to be an effective process.

Although no one will admit it, the interviewer often makes his or her selection based on little more than a gut feeling. In fact, credible research shows that most hiring decisions are made within minutes (see *Blink: The Power of Thinking Without Thinking* by Malcolm Gladwell). The subconscious of the interviewer spends the rest of the interview finding ways to back up his or her initial impression. Even though largely unproven to be effective and seemingly unfair—no employer has found a way to hire that excludes an old fashioned face-to-face interview.

This chapter covers how to truly impress an interviewer and reinforce your status as a star candidate throughout the discussion. It gathers advice from some of the most successful recent hires of our generation who nailed the interviews for their dream job. This chapter will focus on interviewing in general—the final three chapters cover behavioral, technical, and human resource interviews in further detail.

BUILDING AN INTERVIEWING STRATEGY

When preparing for any interview, formulating a general plan defining what information you want the employer to know about you is very important. Although you may be confident that the conversation will be a positive one that markets you well, leaving the discussion to chance by talking about what first comes to mind is never as effective as the performance from a candidate that has prepared an interviewing strategy. Not setting any goals for the information you want to communicate is like beginning a downhill ski race without first becoming familiar with the slopes. A skier that knows the trails and has formed a general plan for navigating them has the advantage.

A candidate should not expect to rely on the interviewer to carry the entire conversation with their questions. The interviewer will certainly steer the discussion, but the majority of the actual talking is done by the person being interviewed. What the candidate chooses to emphasize and how experiences are brought to light can be planned ahead.

So what is the most important information to convey? To answer this question, consider the most important characteristics to employers—as described in *Chapter 1: Building Unmatched Credentials*—passion, an industry perspective, and a results-oriented approach:

Passion

Include any relevant accomplishments that involve passion as part of your interviewing strategy. Think about any past experiences where an interest for your field or sheer passion has resulted in success. Even if not related to your field, such experiences are worth emphasizing.

It is important not only to show that you have passion from past experiences, but also to be passionate during an interview. An average candidate may think of interview questions as problems they are forced to solve, while a star candidate is likely to welcome questions with interest and enthusiasm.

Industry Perspective

Whenever possible, showcase that you have engaged in activities that are related to the industry or business needs of the organization. Be very attentive to any information given by the interviewer regarding what the requirements and working environment are like for the position. Emphasize any experience or characteristics which match the needs of the industry, business, or position.

Results-oriented Approach

It is always best to quantify the results of accomplishments wherever possible. Be ready to talk about your ability to manage resources and lead peers resulting in meeting goals. For example, successfully organizing a team to meet a deadline with limited man-hours and resources could prove to be an impressive experience showcasing a results-oriented approach.

It is recommended that you brainstorm and write down ideas under each of these categories until you have an outline of key information that you want to talk about during an interview. Of course, depending on how structured the interview is, you may not have the chance to emphasize the information you have strategically targeted for the discussion. However, when you are unsure of how to make a point or have the flexibility to steer the conversation, think of the above three key characteristics. You can even mention them directly. Consider the following answer to the common interview question "Can you tell me about yourself?"

Certainly. I grew up in Chicago and chose to attend this university on a scholarship. I'm a civil engineer graduating next December.

*I'm known for my **passion** for innovative structural design encompassing a variety of—what I think to be—fascinating projects ranging from winning a wooden bridge-building competition as a young teen, to my current project that tests which geometric shapes can cut costs when using concrete.*

*I have a strong **industry perspective** considering my internship experience which is how I came up with the idea of researching efficient ways of using building materials.*

My old boss always said "Blake knows how to get things done." I like to focus on **results***, so the added value I bring in my work is clear.*

A response like this is possible during an interview with a prepared interviewing strategy. It is unlikely that a candidate who answers the same question with whatever pops into his or her mind can match the quality of the answer above.

An interview is not a time to be modest. If you don't convey your successes, the employer has no way to distinguish you from other candidates. Preparation is also crucial. Candidates often rationalize that there is no need to prepare because doing so is not "being themselves."

Before giving a speech, do you refuse to prepare because you want to be yourself? There is nothing wrong with *being at your best*. It is important to be yourself and to interview in a style that reflects you; however, if you want to improve your interviewing performance be sure to prepare. It is also vital to prepare by practicing questions and participating in mock interviews. See *Chapter 8: Behavioral Interviews* or *Chapter 9: Technical Interviews* for more information on practicing.

Finally, it is crucial that you know yourself. Spend some time writing down characteristics that describe what you would be like as part of the workforce. If you are hardworking, be sure to develop that quality into your interviewing strategy. If you are a strong communicator with natural social skills try to develop a good way to demonstrate this to the interviewer. Knowing yourself is a vital step in describing your strengths to others.

BEFORE THE INTERVIEW

Spending a little time to make sure everything is in order before an interview can ensure everything goes smoothly. This way you can relax and concentrate on your interviewing strategy instead of stressing out about arriving on time or other details. Consider the following checklist:

- *Make certain that you know the exact location and time of the interview.* If you have not been to the interview site before, physically visit it the day before and keep track of how long it takes to get there. Take a moment to be sure that nothing can come up that would conflict with the arranged time.

- *Memorize the interviewer's name and title.* Try emailing an assistant or receptionist if you are missing the information.

- *Get plenty of rest.* A good night's sleep will put you at your best. A mild sleeping aid such as Tylenol PM can help to prevent a sleepless night due to anticipation.

- *Eat breakfast.* You will need all the energy you can get. Give yourself plenty of time in the morning to enjoy a wholesome breakfast.

- *Research the company.* If you know the specific position, be sure to include it in your search for information. *Chapter 4: Researching an Organization* may serve as a complimentary reference.

- *Prepare questions to ask at the end of your interview.* You can even prepare a written list to glance at during the end of an interview. Refer to the "Closing an Interview" section.

PREPARING AN INTERVIEWING PORTFOLIO

A professional portfolio is certainly worth your time. It is an excellent way to differentiate yourself as few students showcase their accomplishments with a portfolio. It can be especially impressive if you can use a portfolio to illustrate answers to interview questions.

Most ink jet printers support photo quality printing with high gloss paper which is perfect for a portfolio. You can also have one assembled for a modest fee at an office printing service such as Kinko's. Try to keep your portfolio within four to five pages and with as few words as possible considering that the interviewer will only have time to glance at a few images or figures.

Consider the following ideas when deciding what to add to your portfolio:

- *Pictures of anything you have built.* If you have built or assembled a physical engineering/scientific project—such as a model, experiment, machine, or circuit board—it can be an excellent addition to your portfolio.

- *Diagrams of designs.* This can include architectural drawings, graphs, computer system flowcharts, circuit designs, etc.

- *Images of tools.* Pictures of tool use, physical or software based, can serve as valuable additions. For example, Eclipse, Maya, or a soldering iron are good examples of tools.

- *Public speaking.* If you have a picture of yourself giving a talk in front of an audience, it can make a good addition to a portfolio.

- *Self-written case studies.* Personal case studies are becoming very popular for executive-level interviews. They are made up of a few simple paragraphs describing a challenging problem, your solution, and the results (they follow the PAR system as described in "How to Deliver Strong Answers" in Chapter 8). If you have been part of a challenging experience that required making tough decisions with unclear answers you may want to consider writing out a brief case on it with the headings—problem, solution, and results.

  Most college interviewers are not familiar with a self-written case, but they may be useful if the discussion turns to the described experience. If you do encounter someone who also occasionally interviews high-level management, it may prove to be very impressive. When organizations interview a candidate with strong potential, they often schedule an interview with a high-level manager which may be an executive such as a general manager or vice president.

WHAT TO WEAR

Unfortunately, the answer to this question is "it depends." This is especially the case for engineers and scientists; for many other professions, a suit is never a bad choice. What to wear greatly depends on the organization's culture. The golden rule to follow is to be more formal than the general dress code for the organization. This way you match their culture, but still show that you want to impress them.

If jeans with a t-shirt is the norm, consider business casual attire. If an organization's employees often wear business casual attire, pin-striped or solid color formal business wear is appropriate. If they sometimes wear a tie or a jacket, that is a sure sign that a suit is required.

When in doubt call or email someone. If you still are not certain, err on the side of caution and conservatism. It is worse to be under-dressed than overdressed. However, wearing a suit isn't a universal safe choice. It is often the case that highly technical interviewers or research-oriented scientists do not take candidates in suits as seriously.

The following advice should prove useful:

- Do not wear bright colors such as red

- Do not chew gum or smoke

- Make sure your pockets do not have bulges or coins

- Consider using a briefcase or portfolio (black or dark brown)

- Avoid strong cologne or perfume

Men, follow these rules:

- Do not wear jewelry other than a watch or wedding ring

- Make sure you have a clean shaved face or well-groomed facial hair

- Be certain to have clean nails that are trimmed

- Wear dark socks (long enough so legs never show)

- Wear a belt that matches your shoes

Women, consider the following guidelines:

- Do not wear revealing clothing such as mini-skirts

- Dress to be professional rather than "glamorous"

- If you use nail polish, use a clear or conservative color

- If you wear hosiery, use a color which matches your skin

- Do not wear shoes with large heels

- Avoid using a purse (use a briefcase or portfolio instead)

TIPS ON REDUCING NERVOUSNESS

Everyone gets a bit nervous before an important interview. Fortunately, there are some effective measures to take for what is a serious concern—many candidates are chosen simply because of what seems like natural confidence. If you are under the impression that thinking "Relax everything will work out if you try your best" is the only thing you can do to reduce the pressure, consider these tips gathered from some of the finest new-hires of the information age:

- *Become knowledgeable about the organization.* Doing some research can give you an added edge of confidence over other candidates. Company research reduces the unknown which experts agree to be a fundamental cause of anxiety. *Chapter 4: Researching an Organization* may serve as a complementary reference.

- *Practice.* Practice until marketing yourself is second nature. It can only improve your confidence. Refer to "Practice interviewing will give you an edge" and "Sample questions" from *Chapter 8: Behavioral Interviews* for related material.

- *Tell your friends and relatives about interviews only after you have completed them.* Shocked? Take a moment to think about who has the highest expectations for your success. If your loved ones often hold you to a high standard or incessantly gossip about your future, it can add a great deal of pressure while interviewing. Not worrying about how you will tell your parents if you don't get the job can take quite a load off your back. If you decide to use this approach, it will be a peasant surprise to your loved ones when you do get offers.

- *Get safety offers.* There is a big difference between looking for a job and looking for a better job. Having an offer in your pocket can add a sense of security that almost invariably makes a difference.

- *Do something active.* The power of physical activity in reducing stress is very effective according to a wealth of studies. Take a few minutes the morning of the interview to stretch, go for a power walk, rollerblade, or whatever your favorite activity is. If you don't often exercise, more is not necessarily better—attending an interview tired and sore could reflect poorly upon you.

CAMPUS INTERVIEWS

Compared to more formal interviews, such as site interviews, campus interviews are short affairs where you may be little more than a number compared to the other dozen candidates interviewing. The interviewer is likely to take structured notes to better compare the numerous potential hires.

Take advantage of the fact that the interviews are being conducted on your home turf and your university wants it to be the best experience possible for you. Talk to representatives of the organization hosting the interviews at your university. Tell them you have an interview coming up and ask what to expect. Consider the following advice for campus interviews:

- *Find out if there is a "pre-selection" application process.* Many universities post upcoming company interview dates online. Often, students can submit an application for a specific interview listed. This can be very valuable in the event that you cannot attend an employer presentation or university career event. The employer then creates a pre-selected pool of candidates from resumes they have collected from various sources and invite them to interview on-campus.

- *Ask if you can choose your interview slot.* There is often flexibility to choose a time especially when classes are in session and students have busy schedules. The best interview slots are the first, the last, or the slot before lunch. The interviewers are likely to remember you best if you are first or last. If you are right before lunch, they may remember your performance most vividly while discussing the candidates over their meal.

- *Universities often have rules for the employers interviewing.* Many of the rules are there to make campus interviews as positive as possible for you. Such rules can include how long the interviews last and limitations on the types of questions that are allowed. For example, see http://depts.washington.edu/careers/employers from the University of Washington.

PHONE INTERVIEWS

Phone interviews can range from HR screening interviews to two hour long sessions (for example, see http://www.ibm.com/extremeblue). Phone interviews are most popular for internships, because they lower hiring costs. Consider the following when preparing for a phone interview:

- *You can cheat!* Almost any imaginable resource can be available to you during a phone interview. If laying out a cheat sheet of every product the company produces or notes describing each of the keywords on your resume makes you feel more comfortable, then do it.

- *Expect HR interview questions.* It is likely that you will be asked about location preferences, salary, or group preferences during a screening interview. See *Chapter 10: Understanding Human Resources–HR interviews, salary negotiation, & more.*

- *Use a headset.* Headsets for phones are inexpensive and make a difference. This way your hands are free and you can avoid cramps from holding the phone for a prolonged period of time. If you purchase a new headset, be sure to test it with a friend before the interview to ensure it works and the volume is set correctly.

- *You pick the environment.* Find a quiet, familiar place to conduct the interview.

- *Don't ignore physical preparation.* Conducting an interview in your pajamas before showering may sound appealing, but it can lead to an overly-relaxed mood and informal language.

- *Pay attention to time zones.* Make sure that you know the time zone that the interviewer is in. When the call is scheduled ask whether the given time is according to eastern standard time, pacific time, etc.

- *Use a professional voicemail message.* Interviewers may call back for an additional question or they may call at an unexpected time for a variety of reasons. "Leave a message for Princess Layla" may rub them the wrong way.

- *Mark your calendar and notify anyone else who uses the phone.* Even if it's an interview for a safety offer do all you can to ensure your schedule is open.

- *Be sure your cellphone is charged and has good reception at the location.* Are you planning to conduct the interview between classes on your cellphone? Visit your planned spot and check the reception. Think about how you can make sure you fully charge your phone that day.

- *Drink a glass of water before.* Singers often drink nothing other than water before a performance. This can be beneficial as speaking clearly is a requirement.

- *Smile during the conversation.* Smiling has a positive effect on your voice which the interviewer will notice.

- *Get out of your chair.* Standing provides a natural energy and can help to project your voice more clearly.

LUNCH AND DINNER INTERVIEWS

An interview over lunch or dinner is usually in addition to other forms of interviewing. Unless it is for a consulting or sales position, an interview over lunch is usually less rigorous and less significant than an office interview. However, take them seriously; not only are you judged on the discussion, but on how you engage a social situation, how you present yourself, how polite you are, and how you handle a meal. When possible it is always beneficial to eat at the restaurant the day before in order to familiarize yourself with the environment and the menu. At least lookup the menu online beforehand so you can concentrate on more important concerns during the interview. Consider the following guidelines:

- *Wait until the interviewer is seated before you sit.* If you have a jacket follow their lead as well on whether to hand it to a greeter, hang it on your chair, or keep it on.

- *One alcoholic drink or none at all.* An alcoholic drink is only a safe choice if the interviewers order one. If you are invited to order your drink first, there is nothing wrong with asking an interviewer what he or she is ordering before making your decision. Saying something like "I'll have the same" is always a good choice. If you are considering wine, ask the server which house wine would go best with the meal you are considering.

- *Do not assume employers look unfavorably on candidates that are comfortable with a social environment involving alcohol.* For example, client facing representatives often work with decision-makers that like to close deals over a drink. Of course, if you don't drink, you are never at a disadvantage.

- *When the drinks are served, put the napkin on your lap.* If you like, it is appropriate to offer a toast when drinks are served. Be sure to look at the interviewers rather than your glass when making a toast.

- *Order a light meal that is easy to eat.* Pasta or salads are usually good choices. Avoid anything that involves using your hands, cutting, or things like clams, lobster, etc.

- *Do not begin eating until everyone is served.* If your meal is delayed and everyone else is served, it is polite to encourage your interviewers to begin without you.

- *Keep the conversation light while everyone is still eating.* Unless your interviewers actively carry the conversation, let them get a bit of food down first. Gauge how fast you should be eating with respect to the others at the table.

- *Do not insist on paying the bill.* Although it may seem polite, it is well understood that the employer is accommodating you. Instead, thank the interviewers for the meal and the engaging discussion.

CLOSING AN INTERVIEW

If all goes well, the end of the interview is your chance to turn the tables and do a bit of your own interviewing. Always ask questions; it shows that you are motivated and are seriously considering the position.

Be polite and courteous while asking questions. If they dodge a question or don't fully answer it, move on to your next question rather than pushing for unnecessary details. If the interviewer is short on time, ask no more than two short questions.

Here are some excellent questions to consider:

- How did you end up working here?

- Are there any concerns you have or something I haven't touched on that is a key requirement for the position?

- What is a typical day like on the job?

- Why are you hiring?

- Can you give me examples of rising stars in your organization that started in this position?

- What does this position offer that similar positions in my field do not?

If you are excited about the position be sure to say so! Of course, do not plead with them. You may want to say something like "I'm very impressed with the hiring process so far. If someone were to ask me who I hope to work for, your department would certainly be at the top of my list."

Finally, ask for a business card at the end of a site or campus interview. If it's a phone interview, you can ask for their email.

AFTER THE INTERVIEW

Gather any collected business cards and send thank you emails the day of or the day after an interview. It is important to write something genuine in a thank you note. Refer to something interesting you talked about with the interviewer or emphasize how you can be of value to their needs. Make sure the note is short—within two paragraphs.

A thank you note can also serve as a form of damage control. If there clearly was a weakness in your performance or if you said something a little odd, this is a chance to apologize or make things clear in carefully chosen words.

Below are two thank you emails that were actually used by rising stars who contributed to this book:

Subject: Thanks

Aaron,

Thanks for taking the time to interview me today. It was very refreshing compared to run-of-the-mill technical and behavioral interviews I have had in the past. It is clear to me now that your organization provides the opportunity to be challenged unlike any other.

Although my end of the discussion was not as insightful as I had hoped, you should now have an idea of my character and personality. I have a reputation for being passionate and having a "can do" attitude in my professional work. I could not be more impressed with Bain and am proud to have made it even this far.

Best Regards,

First Name

Subject: Thank you for your time

Amitava,

It was a pleasure interviewing with you yesterday. It was fascinating to hear your insights regarding the airline industry. The experience has left quite an impression on me. I appreciate your honest and direct advice—I think it helped to give me a better perspective of IBM Business Consulting Services. I hope we have the chance to work together.

Sincerely,

First Name

After two weeks it is appropriate to write a follow-up note. It should be very brief mentioning the date you interviewed and any upcoming deadlines you have. Here is an example:

Subject: Interview follow-up

It was my pleasure interviewing with Google Thursday the 14th. If I failed to mention it earlier I apologize—my expected graduation date is this December. There are no pressing deadlines as of yet; I would just like to touch base and see if there is any other information you need in order to make a decision.

Sincerely,

First Name

COMMON MISTAKES

1. *Being late.* If you suspect you will be late, call.

2. *Not taking scheduling seriously.* When setting up a date for an interview, be sure to check you don't have an exam or family event on the potential date.

3. *Not researching the company.* Company research is important to boost your confidence and for having engaging conversations during interviews.

4. *Not letting the interviewer lead.* Be a good listener and always let them finish their thoughts before speaking.

5. *Talking about salary or benefits.* Even if the interviewer brings it up, avoid the subject with something like "To tell you the truth, I haven't done any research on my expectations of salary yet" which should indeed be the truth. See chapter *Chapter 10: Understanding Human Resources—HR interviews, salary negotiation, & more for more information.*

6. *Leaving a cell phone ringer on.* Murphy's law applies to interviews; your phone can and will ring at the worst possible time with the most inappropriate ring tone.

7. *Informal beginnings.* Be sure to shake the interviewer's hand and wait to be seated.

8. *Inappropriate appearance.* See the "What to wear" section for suggestions. Additionally, check your appearance in the restroom between interviews and after lunch.

Profile
Rhett Aultman

You're in a bit of a different situation than the other contributors to this book—is that correct?

Yes, I just finished a whirlwind tour of interviewing and am deciding among Amazon, Microsoft, and Google for a summer internship. They are all software development positions and are all, by coincidence, in Washington state—located in Seattle, Redmond, and Kirkland respectively.

What's on your mind? How are you basing your decision?

Well, considering they are internships, I suspect the monetary compensation is comparable. So, what's mainly on my mind is the opportunity the positions can give me in the future, how interested I am in the technology the positions involve, and whether the experience would fit well with my Ph.D. research. It's not an easy decision, every company offered something a bit different:

In my opinion, Amazon has the most hands-on technical challenge of the bunch. They were very receptive to tailoring a position for me by providing a list of active projects and allowing me to choose the three of most interest. Amazon also hinted at the possibility of finding something that would fit well as a doctoral thesis topic.

The Microsoft interviews mainly regarded XML, SOAP, web services, enterprise interoperability and such. They also do some work with COM and COM+. It's definitely interesting because those technologies are in mainstream tech news almost daily.

Google offers a bunch of intangibles such as my favorite location out of the three, a trendier name, and lots of free stuff. Originally, the position they offered me was a little weaker in comparison with the others as far as interesting technology. However, they were very flexible after I talked with them a bit about it. They changed the position to one involving Jabber which is a chat interface and work in founding a new Google Labs project.

How did you get all these interviews?

Microsoft and Amazon attended a college career fair at my university. Amazon was all about having a technical discussion right from the start. Even at the booth I had a discussion about the challenges of dealing with enormous databases in addition to where my interests lie. I applied at Google through their website. I also have a friend that works there which helped I think.

Did you research the companies?

Some companies definitely make it easier than others. For Microsoft, I did the standard review of their college website and looked at their latest research projects. Knowing about their technology on the fringe that hasn't gotten a lot of press definitely helped me to be more enthusiastic than other candidates.

Amazon was a lot tougher. For example, I had to resort to the website of the real estate agency that handles their lease to find out what their buildings look like. Google was a bit easier because they provide information on their corporate life, current active projects, and technologies on Google Labs.

How do you approach interviewing?

What has been invaluable for me is just chatting with friends in my field. It can be so helpful to practice chatting with people who are competent in general, work in different areas of your field, and enjoy an open discussion. Whenever you have time and the environment encourages it, bounce around open ideas with your friends.

I also think it is important to speak your mind while interviewing even if you aren't sure how to solve a problem. I don't know how many times I have come up with an answer to a question that I knew to be less than perfect and said something like "I don't have proof that I can't do better, but I suspect the solution could be improved if I thought about it a little more."

Have any memorable questions?

During an interview with Amazon, I was asked a technical question which I started to answer with a popular programming language. Halfway through, I thought I could use a functional language called ML which is rarely used in industry, but sometimes used in research or for teaching. I suspected that the interviewer would be familiar with it because he had mentioned a functional language previously called LISP.

Boy did his eyes light up. "Really!" he said. So, my hunch was correct that he preferred functional languages over the more popular languages of today and I scrambled to try and rewrite the problem. What's interesting is I never got around to finishing the solution, but I think my little attempt and our discussion was the most favorable part of the interview.

Have any of your interviews been something other than office interviews?

Yes. I had some lunch interviews as well. They were more casual with engineering discussions and a few brain teasers here and there.

My advice for a lunch interview would be to pick what you eat carefully. Try to pick food that won't embarrass you! Also, avoid anything that will take unnecessary attention and can keep you from talking. You may want to pay attention to what your interviewer gets, because if he or she is vegetarian, a 20oz steak could affect their perception of you. Also, try to avoid carbohydrate shock; you'll need to be alert for the rest of your interviews. One thing that works for me is a caffeine boost. In my case, a few glasses of iced tea make my mental capacities infinitely clearer.

What advice would you give someone who is about to have a big interview?

I like to get my mind going—I usually bring some related material to read. It's very important to know the company's products as well. If you are expecting technical interviews, be sure to brush up on the fundamentals of your field. I like to go over some basic computer algorithms before interviews.

Finally, the most important thing is to relax. The interviewers just want to know what you're like. Think of it as a typical engineering discussion with a friend. Knock down the illusion that the people you will speak with are adversarial. You aren't going to war here. They are just regular people who are looking for someone to help them with their projects.

What would you do different if you could do it all over again?

I think I would have been more selective in designing my resume. I now realize it is important to emphasize what you are most interested in rather than listing everything you can. It plays a big role when companies match a candidate to a team. After the interviews are done, you leave, but the resume stays.

I wish I had gone to grad school straight out of undergrad. I think if you are passionate about your field and plan to spend the rest of your life in it, there is no better place to be. I don't regret my time working after undergrad which certainly made me a pretty penny, but things get so much more interesting with the knowledge of a quality graduate education. Now that I'm in grad school everyone takes me a lot more seriously, there are more interesting things to work on, and opportunities present themselves which simply didn't exist before.

James "Rhett" Aultman

121 SE 16th Ave #J303
Gainesville, FL 32601
Phone: 352.338.9260 E-mail: wlight@weatherlight.com

EDUCATION

University of Florida, CISE Department — Current
Ph.D student, estimated date of graduation: Spring 2007

University of Florida, Warrington College of Business Administration — 2001
BSBA in Computer Science

PROFESSIONAL EXPERIENCE

CISE Department, University of Florida — January 2004-Present
Teaching Assistant
Teaching assistant for COP4600: *Principles of Operating Systems.* Responsible for development of curriculum through the creation of assignments and projects, teaching discussion sections each week, and holding office hours to interface with and tutor students. As the coordinating TA for the staff, additional duties included taking responsibility for the quality of the course and for supervising and coordinating the efforts of the staff. Curriculum has focused around the development of new features for the MINIX operating system

FCCI Insurance Group — August 2003-December 2003
Contractor
Responsibilities, duties, and projects all extensions of previous responsibilities, duties, and projects during time as an Applications Software Developer II with FCCI Insurance Group.

FCCI Insurance Group — October 2001-August 2003
Applications Software Developer II
Responsible for development and maintenance of business technology solutions utilized both internally and by external customers. Projects employ a wide range of Java technology, including Servlets, JSP, EJB, and Java Web Start GUI applications. Technologies also used include XML, XSLT, XSL Formatting Objects (Apache FOP Parser), and Apache Velocity. Development environment employed Eclipse IDE, Oracle and DB/2 databases, and AS/400 mainframe integration tools. Further responsibilities include representation of the team in the open source communities responsible for the JBoss J2EE server and the Apache Formatting Objects Processor.

Weatherlight Technologies — April 1999-Present
Senior Lead Developer
Responsible for developing various forms of open-source, freeware, and commercial software. Projects have employed a wide array of different technologies, including Perl, Java, Java Servlets, XML, J2EE and web-based architectures. Projects developed on heterogeneous network of Windows, Solaris, and Linux machines using Oracle8i as primary database and JBoss J2EE server. In addition, responsible for other Weatherlight Technologies services such as Endymion Mailman installation and customization services. Projects include
- Weatherlight Dynamic Content Generator
- Swagger instant messenger client
- Swagger instant messaging API
- JabberBots automated instant messenger services framework.

Endymion Corporation — April 1999-May 2001
Responsible for non-development technical activities and primary technical customer relations. In charge of supporting, testing, debugging, and customizing company products (web-based email solutions). Utilized Perl, CGI, Java Servlets, and the HTTP, POP, and SMTP protocols. Also responsible for maintenance of documentation, including moving multiple documentation formats to a single XML standard as well as a project to provide on-line support.

Marston Science Library, University of Florida — February 1999-August 1999
Technical Assistant
Provided support for a network utilizing TCP/IP, Windows Networking, and Novell Netware. Responsible for the proper setup, configuration, and troubleshooting of user software as well as for the proper management and maintenance of the 150 Windows and MacOS client machines used both by library staff and by library patrons in a public lab environment.

PUBLICATIONS

"JVMPI: Java Virtual Machine Profiling Interface" *Java Developers' Journal* 8(2) 2003, pp. 30-34.
"XML and IM: Instant Messaging with Jabber" *XML Journal* 3(7) 2002, pp. 16-17.

PRESENTATIONS

JINI Distributed Network Services. Suncoast Java Users' Group, Sarasota FL, October 2002.
Aspect Oriented Programming. Suncoast Java Users' Group, Sarasota FL., January 2003.
JNI And JVMPI: Native Code In Java Suncoast Java Users' Group, Sarasota FL, February 2003.

RESEARCH

- Data and content organization over dynamic federated systems and models of programming to exploit parallelism and data ubiquity. (Proposed Thesis Topic)
- Efficient mechanisms for the general-case detection of cheating in distributed computations (Term project, CEN6505: Computer Communication Networks)
- Survey of effective garbage collection techniques and the interface between programming languages and garbage collection systems. Part of an independent study supervised by Dr. Michael Frank. (http://www.livejournal.com/users/gc_study)
- Development of compiled, statically typed programming language for image manipulation. (Course project, COP5555: Programming Language Principles)
- Extensions to the Jabber messaging protocol (http://www.jabber.org) with a focus on distributed services construction.
- Entropy growth with respect to time in the Critters cellular automata, demonstrating the bijective nature of entropy in a reversible system. (http://www.weatherlight.com/critters)
- Detection of constraints in an FO document that prevent any possible layout. Part of the Apache FOP project.
- Performance profiling for a J2EE server at runtime with a focus on leveraging AOP techniques for real-time profiling.

TECHNICAL KNOWLEDGE

Java, C, C++, Perl, x86 Assembly (NASM and AT&T Syntax), Visual Basic, CGI, PL/SQL, Sybase, Oracle, Linux, UNIX, WinNT/Win2K, Apache Tomcat, Apache Velocity, Apache Jetspeed, Apache FOP, JRUN, XML, XSL, VoiceXML, WAP/WML, HTML, network administration, operating systems.

8

Behavioral Interviews

Behavioral interviews are by far the most common type of interviews. Even rigorous technical interviews or HR screening interviews often mix in a few behavioral questions probing your past experiences or to test if your values are in-line with the organization's culture. This chapter describes what to expect, how to prepare, and how to deliver an unmatched performance during a behavioral interview.

The reader is encouraged to read the profiles appended to each chapter in addition to the advice in this chapter. Nearly every rising star profiled discusses their interviewing experiences.

THE PURPOSE BEHIND BEHAVIORAL INTERVIEWS

Behavioral interviews study past behavior. The assumption made by employers is that future behavior reflects past behavior. Questions that evaluate values such as ethics, leadership, motivation, and social behavior are also considered behavioral questions.

Passion, an industry perspective, and being results-oriented, the three characteristics discussed in "Building an interviewing strategy" of *Chapter 7: Learning the Art of Interviewing*, should serve as the corner stones for values to emphasize in behavioral interviews. However, what other types of qualities an organization is specifically looking for depends on the company's culture and often varies with each interviewer. For example, willingness to travel or working in large teams may be key characteristics to an organization.

Company research can be crucial in finding out what an organization is looking for in a behavioral interview. Companies such as General Electric and Ford Motors often have very formal scripted behavioral interviews for college candidates which involve a point system. If you can find information related to their interviewing format—for example, through an industry insider (as described in "Getting the insider view" of *Chapter 4: Researching an Organization*)—it is likely that future interviews from that organization will be consistent.

How to Prepare

The key to mastering behavioral interviews is understanding that every behavioral question will map to one or more of your past experiences. If you are proficient at verbally showcasing past situations and accomplishments, answers to corresponding behavioral questions become far more impressive. You cannot predict what will be asked during an interview, but you can prepare a toolkit of familiar experiences to handle any behavioral question with complete confidence and composure.

You should begin preparing by brainstorming the content of your behavioral interviewing toolkit. Compile a list of past experiences and accomplishments that cover a wide range of situations. It should be in line with your interviewing strategy. Look for situations that involve passion, an industry perspective, a results-oriented approach, innovation, motivation, challenging situations, group experiences, goals that would not have succeeded without your efforts, and tests of your ethics.

A resume is a good place to start, but some of the best material for behavioral interviews comes from outside of academic and industry related experience. For example, organizing a choir performance for church may be a strong addition to your toolkit. The list should be roughly between five and ten past experiences.

Once you have a clear understanding of which experiences are best to talk about during your interviews, practice describing them. Interviewing is very similar to public speaking without notes or slides—interviewing is a performance. A good public speaker not only is comfortable in front of the audience, but also delivers an honest, natural performance because he or she is very familiar with the subject matter. Describing your past experiences needs to be second nature.

It is recommended that you practice talking about your experiences out-load. Consider painting a picture of yourself—starting from your high school days all the way to the present—describing the key experiences in your toolkit throughout that timeline. Tape recording your descriptions is also beneficial.

At first, the mini-speeches will be rather unorganized stories where you don't immediately find the best way to convey the information. This is, in fact, how many candidates perform during interviews. However, as you fine-tune your descriptions of past situations and accomplishments, communicating them becomes a confident performance that is second nature.

As an example of a description for an experience in a behavioral interviewing toolkit, consider the following description of an internship:

> *I interned as a database administrator last summer which is an experience that will be an asset to my career. I was assigned to evaluate and research the addition of a new database. It was an ambition project because it needed to span the entire organization including the finance, accounting, production, and development divisions. Management was unsure how such a database could be designed. I was assigned to lay out the groundwork for more senior engineers.*

> *I saw this as an opportunity to bring even greater value to their business. After diligent research on database design and after taking the initiative to talk to experts inside the organization, spanning low level engineers to financial officers, I wrote a proposal for how the database should be implemented. Then I further exceeded their expectations, by building a working prototype to serve as the foundation for what is now a successful addition to their IT infrastructure. By the end of the internship, I had built a working system going beyond the call of duty which was just to turn in a research paper.*

This description touches on a variety of characteristics that often arise in behavioral interviews. For example, the experience could be used to answer questions about motivation, self-initiative, communication, meeting deadlines, learning quickly through research, and utilizing help from others. Of course, this would only be one accomplishment in the candidates toolkit, it is not as strong of a fit for behavioral questions regarding team experiences, ethical situations, or leadership.

Finally, it is important to understand that this form of preparing is not memorizing. If you find yourself writing down a script and memorizing it like a real speech, your time is not being spent in the most productive way. How you describe past experiences will be different for every behavioral interview—it cannot be memorized. The goal of this type of preparing is to master describing past experiences so talking about them is very familiar and can be done with a natural confidence.

PRACTICE WILL GIVE YOU AN EDGE

Once you have a toolkit of experiences to draw from, it is recommended that you practice using that toolkit for behavioral questions. Keep in mind that knowing the answers to specific questions isn't as important as becoming adept at mapping your past experiences to different questions. The sample behavioral interview and sample questions at the end of this chapter should prove useful for practicing. Additionally, a quick search online should yield more than enough behavioral questions for your needs.

There is no better practice than the real thing. It is recommended that you interview anywhere and everywhere. Not only can you practice your interviewing technique, but learn about an organization related to your field, build your network, and explore different types of positions and roles. It can also yield "safety offers" and give you a perspective on what you are worth (see *Chapter 10: Understanding Human Resources—HR interviews, salary negotiation, & more*).

The next best thing is to conduct a mock interview. University career counselors often specialize in giving mock behavioral interviews. If you have friends that have interned for the organization or one of its competitors, it can be especially beneficial. If you want to get the most out of the experience possible, video tape the session. It is an effective way to evaluate what you need to work on to improve your interviewing technique.

How to Deliver Strong Answers

The previous sections cover how to prepare for behavioral interviews, but how do you nail the questions during the actual interview? Consider the following advice for specific types of behavioral questions:

Situational Questions

Most behavioral questions are situational. A situational question is a behavioral question that asks you to describe a situation from your past which meets certain parameters. The first step in answering a situational question is choosing which past experience to base your answer on.

If you can't immediately decide between past events, feel free to ask the interviewer which experience they would prefer to hear about. If you have prepared a diverse toolkit of experiences, it is unlikely you will encounter a behavioral question you cannot map to an experience immediately; however, if you are having trouble picking a relevant past experience, you should have some flexibility to use a similar situation. For example, if you are asked to talk about a time you failed to accomplish a goal you could say something like "I'm afraid I don't have a very good example of this, but I do have an example of a situation that nearly failed until I intervened."

PAR or **P**roblem-**A**ction-**R**esult (also known as STAR or Situation-Task-Action-Result) is a system which can help to organize a strong answer to a situational question. It is important to become familiar with this approach since many organizations utilize the PAR system to formally evaluate interview answers. While describing your experiences be sure you clearly cover the problem, action, and result. PAR can also serve as a check at the end of an answer to make sure everything relevant has been covered. If it makes you more comfortable, feel free to divide your answer into three modular segments stating problem, action, and result literally. Consider this example:

Interviewer: Tell me about a time when you took initiative.

*Candidate: Certainly. The **problem** I was faced with was that my professor was running out of funding for a research project I was working on in the area of metal durability.*

*I really enjoyed the work and felt it to be novel, so I immediately took **action** by researching who else would be interested in our findings. I knew my professor always sought funding from academic sources such as the National Science Foundation, so I targeted industry in my search instead.*

*The **results** were remarkable. After a few proposals to the auto industry and aerospace industry, we received multiple sources of funding. I presented the findings at a conference in Chicago and the data has been published in many industry magazines.*

Team Questions

Although a subset of situational questions, group questions come up so often in behavioral interviews that they deserve special attention. Team questions probe your previous experiences working in groups. What the interviewer is specifically looking for varies from organization to organization. For example, they may be evaluating how you would fit in a "virtual team" environment or they be evaluating how you would fit in a team with older, more experienced, members.

A common mistake in answering team-related questions is only emphasizing leadership skills. Leading a team is not something many new hires do in entry-level positions. Emphasizing only leadership when a team question is asked may give the interviewer the impression that you are not very humble or are not willing to start at the bottom to learn.

Experiences that involve working with unskilled or unmotivated team members can often serve as the most impressive answers to team questions. Exceeding expectations while working individually is certainly respectable, but having the ability to influence others to drive results is far more valuable to an organization. Consider this example based on a true story:

***Interviewer:** Can you give me an example of previous work in a group?*

***Candidate:** Yes. I was assigned to a group in a graduate database course. It was an interesting situation because the most senior member of our team seemed very unmotivated. It was clear from the start that he wanted to do the least amount of work possible.*

Instead of assuming the rest of us would need to pick up the slack, I sat next to him during class and got to know him a little better. It soon became clear to me that the reason he wasn't doing much work was a matter of pride. He was a Ph.D. student and didn't want to admit that he didn't know the first thing about the database system we were using.

After I realized this, I lent him one of my favorite books on the subject and high-lighted the most important sections to get him up to speed. I also allowed him to make the ultimate decisions for his part of the project giving him ownership. I think this played well with his personality and allowed him to "save face."

We were chosen to present our project in front of the class. Its success was far better than what would have resulted without his contributions. In fact, I don't think anyone else in the group worked as hard as he did.

Negative Questions

A negative question seeks to find undesirable characteristics about you. They are not trick questions—their motives are usually literally in the question. Be as positive as possible when answering these questions. If you do mention something negative, always explain that you are very aware of the negative characteristic and have a strategy to overcome it. The best approach is to find a way to turn your answer into a favorable quality, value, or characteristic. The following example is based on an answer used by one of the contributors to this book during an interview:

Interviewer: *What is your greatest weakness?*

Candidate: *I'm very passionate about my field and pride myself on elegant, innovative solutions. I often find myself spending a great deal of time challenging the orthodox approach to problems. However, I am very aware of this and make certain that the only result of my curiosity is that more of my personal time goes toward interests in my field. For example, I would never challenge the opinion of a more senior engineer just for the sake of argument.*

Open-ended Questions

If an interviewer asks an open-ended question, there is no expectation of a specific answer. Few students see the opportunity that open-ended questions provide—complete freedom to talk about nearly anything in your toolkit of experiences. These questions are where a bit of preparation can really be beneficial. For ideas on what to emphasize during open-ended questions, refer to "Building an Interviewing Strategy" in Chapter 7. The following sample answer was used during real interviews by a computer scientist. It should be clear that its contributor has a passion for his field.

Interviewer: Why did you choose your area of study?

Candidate: I made up my mind at a very early age. When I was 14, I built a video game with my best friend and I immediately recognized the opportunity software development provides. With just keystrokes you can realize your dreams in computer science. If you have an interesting idea, you can put it in motion without real constraints or resources compared to other fields. Imagine if you wanted to be an architect at the age of 14; what could you hope to do at that age? Perhaps create some drawings? You wouldn't be able to realize your dream of a towering building for at least a decade.

I think of computer science as a form of art. When I see the work of someone in my field, I see that person's character, innovation, and style. Where else can you find such intellectual art? You may say writing or mathematics, but this is not a novel and this is not theory—this is what is driving the information age whether you are crafting a network to carry valuable data, reducing complexity from someone's life, or controlling a space craft.

Hypothetical questions

A hypothetical question such as "If you could be any animal, what would you be?" supposedly tests your personality. What the above question is really asking is "What type of person are you?" When dealing with hypothetical questions, try to answer in line with your interviewing strategy as described in "Building an interviewing strategy" in Chapter 7. Hypothetical questions tend to be a little unusual; it is perfectly fine to take a moment to think about a strong answer. Consider the following example:

Interviewer: If you had $5,000 what would you do with it?

Candidate: To be honest, I would pay off some college loans, but if I had no financial obligations, I would use it to build a file server. I'd love to have a server that is accessible wherever I am to store and backup my important personal files and digital pictures. I'd enjoy setting something like that up considering I'm kind of a "do it yourself" type of person.

Why is this a strong answer? Well, it's not a strong answer under all circumstances. The employer may not necessarily appreciate someone who enjoys tinkering with technology or building things on their own initiative because their top criteria may be communication or team-work. However, if they are looking for someone to work in a hands-on engineering environment with a "can do" attitude, this could be a very impressive answer compared to "I'd buy a new car."

QUICK WAYS TO SHARPEN YOUR INTERVIEWING TECHNIQUE

Consider the following advice for interviews:

- *Listen.* Carefully listen to every word an interviewer says. Perhaps even more importantly, be aware of the interviewer's body language. If you are a good listener, you can determine what information is most relevant to the interviewer and whether your answers are in line with his or her expectations.

- *If you don't know something, admit it.* If anything, the interviewer will be impressed with your honestly—candidates often guess or try to make something up if they don't know the answer to a question. Of course, just saying "I don't know" isn't appropriate. You may want to say something like "The subject sounds familiar, but it is not something I've worked with in my past experience." In the case where you know related information, you can say something like "I don't know a great deal about the Linux kernel, but I use the Linux operating system extensively."

- *If you don't understand a question, repeat it back to them.* Interviewers sometimes poorly word questions. Feel free to confirm what they are asking by repeating the question back to them. Also, if you miss part of the question, don't be afraid to ask them to repeat it.

- *Ask for more information if you need it.* There is no guarantee that an interviewer can give you more details, but there is no harm in politely asking. However, if it is an open-ended question, never ask for specifics because it limits your freedom to answer the question. If you ask for specifics during an open-ended question it can show a lack of confidence or initiative.

- *Never show indecision.* It is perfectly fine to take your time before answering a question, but it is not okay to verbally alternate between two answers during an interview. You can, however, try asking the interviewer for his or her recommendation between two approaches. If no direction is suggested, pick a solution arbitrarily and focus on your logic rather than the solution. In other words, think out-loud. How you think is far more important than whether you are right or wrong in most situations.

- *Pick a facial feature to focus on such as their left eye.* Many people forget entirely how to act comfortably during an interview and find themselves staring at a wall rather than the interviewer while answering questions. Fortunately, you read this book so you won't be ruled out as a weird one. Of course, if you prefer, you can focus on their right eye or their nose.

- *Practice how you will sit.* It may sound silly, but practicing such that you look professional and are comfortable is important. If you decide to video tape a mock interview, it can be insightful to see how professional and comfortable you look while interviewing.

DEALING WITH DIFFERENT INTERVIEWER STYLES

Many interviewers are very good communicators and carry the discussion to make it as positive of an experience as possible. There are, however, different interviewing styles which can present additional challenges to the candidate:

The Silent Treatment

This style is characterized by an interviewer that gives you virtually no feedback in words or body language. The interviewer makes it nearly impossible to read whether you are doing well or not. Sometimes organizations use a "good cop, bad cop" approach to their interviewing where one interview is very friendly and encouraging while the following interview is very stringent and serious.

A common technique used by reporters, is often part of this interviewing style where the interviewer is deliberately silent after your answer. The natural response to the awkward silence is to try and speak more, even if you have completed your thoughts. It can lead to rambling or unnecessary additional information. Instead of falling into this trap, you can end your answers by saying something like "I hope I answered your question."

If you do encounter one of these "stone cold" interviewers, the most important thing to realize is that he or she will not give you any form of immediate feedback on your performance. Do not mistake their silence as negative feedback. It is likely that the interviewer acts in this manner for all candidates. Knowing this can give you an advantage, as many candidates may fear they have made a poor impression on the interviewer from the beginning.

In the case of this interviewing style, the interview is closer to a collection of speeches rather than a discussion. If you have prepared and are familiar with your toolkit of past experiences, answer the questions with the same positive energy and confidence you use while practicing. Continue to make the assumption that you are indeed a star candidate in the interviewer's eyes—even if you are not receiving positive feedback.

The Lecturer

This style is often used by a senior manager, engineer, or scientist. The interviewer is quick to show that he or she is an authority and expert. If a significant amount of time during an interview is used by the interviewer to teach you about their area of expertise and philosophy, you have encountered an interviewer with a lecturing style.

Candidates sometimes respond to this interviewing style by challenging the interviewer's authority. You may feel that you want to show the interviewer that you are as knowledgeable and talented as they are. This can be a dangerous approach as the interviewer is used to being in the position of a mentor and does indeed have authority over the interview to make a positive or negative recommendation. Challenging the interviewer, even if you are certain your observations are correct or you feel your opinion is innovative, can backfire leaving a bad impression.

The best approach is to realize that they are most comfortable in the position of a teacher or mentor. Try to immediately acknowledge their more experienced background and consider yourself their student for the session.

It is important to be humble, but do not take it to the extreme of blindly agreeing with everything they say. Simply praising them and agreeing does not reflect well on your knowledge and intelligence. Instead, add to the discussion and ask for their advice whenever possible to show you are knowledgeable and insightful while keeping the position of a pupil. For example, if you disagree with a point, instead of saying the interviewer is wrong, you can say something like "From your story, I certainly see that teamwork is a vital part of success in our field. I'm curious—what is your opinion on ethics being important for this position considering that issues like the Worldcom and Enron scandals are in the news almost daily."

Unprepared Interviewer

It is often the case that an interviewer has not even prepared questions beforehand, especially when the interviewer is a manager that is very busy. Signs of an unprepared interviewer are when they take a moment to look over your resume at the beginning, do not focus much on the time since they do not have a list of questions that they must go over, ask questions depending on where the discussion goes, and ask a series of open-ended questions like "Can you tell me about yourself?"

Unstructured interviews give you a very strong advantage over other candidates if you have prepared. Since you have more influence on where the discussion goes, you can bring up issues you have researched such as where the strategy of the organization is going, who you think the winners in their market will be in the future, and the strengths and weaknesses of their product portfolio. Additionally, you can emphasize your past experiences and accomplishments in the light you prefer, namely—showcasing passion, an industry perspective, a result-oriented approach, and your best past experiences from your prepared toolkit.

Connecting with an Interviewer

In order to connect with an interviewer, unlike the other candidates, you need to be able to focus on what they are passionate about. It is not an easy task as it requires reading people quickly from what they say and how they behave, as well as an arsenal of knowledge regarding the company's business.

A pattern has emerged from the contributed interviewing experiences studied for this book. Depending on the organization's culture and the background of the individual, most interviewers are focused in one of the following ways:

- *Mission or cause-focused.* In this case, the company culture is driven toward a specific cause or mission. This mission dictates the strategy of the organization and is more important than business goals. For example, Google is known for advocating the cause of making electronic information available in innovative and manageable ways. It can be beneficial to show how your background is in line with such a mission.

- *Business-focused.* Here, business goals such as the value to clients, differentiation, and the organization's business model are of paramount concern. In this case, you should focus on how you can help the organization achieve its business goals.

- *Craft-focused.* A craft focused interviewer is looking for the candidate with the best skills available. Technical interviews are nearly always craft-focused (see *Chapter 9: Technical Interviews*).

These are just guidelines, an interviewer may be focused on a mix of the ideas listed above. However, connecting on the right level and sharing the moment can be the deciding factor for interviews.

AN EXAMPLE BEHAVIORAL INTERVIEW

Interviewer: *It's a pleasure to finally meet you Lauren. I've been looking forward to talking with you.*

Candidate: *Thank you—I'm excited to be here.*

Interviewer: *Just to give you an overview of what is to come, we have about an hour where we'll have a discussion on your past experiences and some of the interesting things you would have the opportunity to do in this position. If you need to take a break or have a question feel free to let me know.*

Candidate: *Thanks—I'll keep that in mind.*

Interviewer: *Great. Let's get started. Why do you want to work for us?*

Candidate: *It is my preference to work for a small company where I have more freedom and a closer relationship with the other members of the organization. I believe in your products—I just bought your latest mp3 player. I follow the consumer electronics industry and was just reading an article in The Wall Street Journal about how this industry has had consistent increases in demand for nearly three decades. I see an opportunity to make a difference and to start my career in a growing industry.*

Interviewer: *Good. Can you tell me about your co-op experience?*

Candidate: *Of course. I worked as an assistant to a senior engineer in writing requirements for various software development projects. We were often referred to as the "customer" for these projects. I learned a great deal about formal software development cycles including the capability maturity model (CMM), creating flowcharts for large systems with UML, and creating requirement documentation.*

After learning the groundwork for writing requirements, I took the initiative to survey which previous requirement documentation had resulted in successful projects. I did this in my spare time, always putting the work assigned to me first on my priority list. After a few weeks of gathering data from various experts within the organization, records, and databases—I found that some projects failed because the requirements were rigid and often did not reflect the needs of the ultimate end user for the software.

I wrote a proposal to my superiors to include feedback from end users and to allow requirements to evolve throughout the software development process. I put up a simple website to facilitate the process that reduced the additional paper-work needed. I then tested the new approach on two upcoming projects.

The "customers" under the proposed process were the end users, not us. There was some resistance within the organization to the new ideas, but I made sure to help and make the process for the engineers on the projects as easy as possible. The positive results were obvious—the projects finished below budget and the end users in the accounting division immediately praised the usefulness of the software. The organization has fully adopted the practices I helped found.

Interviewer: *Give me just a moment while I get all of that down in my notes. Can you give me an example of a time when you had to meet a stringent deadline?*

Candidate: *Yes I can. Nearly half of my grade in a graphics course was a project with a six-week deadline. We had a lot of freedom to choose our topic so I picked a 3-D graphics engine using an open source framework.*

From the beginning, I was concerned about the deadline, so I put up an online journal detailing my daily progress. It is my belief that the level of communication between a superior and a subordinate should be so open that the superior knows when a project will not meet its schedule before the actual person working on it, because of his or her perspective and experience. The blog was my channel for this type of communication. Whenever there was an interest in my project, the professor could immediately check on it at his convenience.

It was my way of providing proof that I had worked hard the entire time. I was fortunate to have my professor read it periodically. It even became semi-famous within the online blogosphere. I didn't finish by the deadline, but since my professor, and the rest of the class for that matter, were well aware of my efforts, I received an A and some bonus credit.

Interviewer: *Can you give me an example of when you were faced with something unknown such as an assignment that required the use of tools you were unfamiliar with?*

Candidate: *Certainly. If I were easily discouraged by unfamiliar tools, I don't think I would have made it through college! I try to find someone who has mastery in the subject when learning something new. It may be an expert in the area, frequent posters on web forums, or an author of a book. I'm never afraid to ask for help; I think our field is so rich and has so much depth that no one can get by without some guidance.*

The best example of this was during the graphics project I mentioned. The entire area of graphics was relatively new to me, so I spent a lot of time talking to my professor, reading, posting threads on news groups, emailing authors of papers, and talking to my peers about the subject. I certainly have experience learning new things in a short period of time.

Interviewer: *Why should we hire you?*

Candidate: *I'm determined to bring great value to your organization, I'm passionate about the field the position is in, I think I have a mature understanding of software development compared to my peers, and I have a track record which proves I drive results.*

Interviewer: *Very good; well, that takes care of my questions. As I mentioned in the beginning, I want to talk a little bit about the position. It is an engineering position where you would be in a group of about six to ten people with a mix of age groups. As you know, the position will be in our main campus in Austin, Texas and is an entry-level position targeting college students. We offer a rotation program where you are exposed to a variety of different technologies and groups within your first year. We have a few more minutes; do you have any questions for me?* [refer to "Closing an interview" of *Chapter 7: Learning the Art of Interviewing* for questions to ask at the end of an interview]

QUESTIONS TO PRACTICE

In addition to the questions showcased in the profiles and the questions mentioned previously in this chapter, here are some common behavioral questions:

- Why did you chose the university you attended?

- Can you tell me a bit about yourself?

- Describe your most challenging experience to date.

- Can you describe a time you failed?

- Rate yourself from 1-5 as an employee.

- Can you describe a situation where you were a leader?

- Describe a conflict in a team that you resolved.

- Do you consider yourself a follower or a leader?

- Have you been in a situation where you used strong communication skills?

- Tell me about a time where you went above and beyond the call of duty.

- Describe a past experience where you had to adapt to your environment.

- If you could have any job in the world, what would it be?

- What is your five year plan?

THE BARE MINIMUM TO DO

The following steps describe the bare minimum to do assuming you have a week before a serious behavioral interview:

1. *List characteristics you want to emphasize (30 min.).* This is covered in "Building an Interviewing Strategy" in Chapter 7. It is important to be familiar with your strongest qualities and what you believe in.

2. *Prepare a toolkit of past experiences to draw upon (30 min.).* As described in "How to prepare," try to develop a set of past experiences and accomplishments that cover a wide range of situations.

3. *Practice talking about your experiences out-loud (2 hours).* It is critical that you become comfortable with marketing your past experiences. It is not something we do often in everyday life; thus, a bit of practice can give you a significant advantage.

4. *Practice mapping your experiences to answers to behavioral questions (2 hours).* Practice with any behavioral questions you can find. As described in "Practice interviewing will give you an edge," remembering the answer to a particular behavioral question is not as important as practicing making a match between a past experience from your toolkit and the question.

5. *Conduct a mock interview at your university career resource center (1 hour).* Peers that have interned for a related organization or a professor can often provide excellent mock interviews as well. This is especially recommended if the upcoming interview is your first.

6. *Do some company research (2+ hours).* Try to find sources of information other than just the company's website. *Chapter 4: Researching an Organization* should serve as a guide.

COMMON MISTAKES

The following list describes common mistakes made during behavioral interviews. It is recommended that you review the common mistakes section of *Chapter 7: Learning the Art of Interviewing* as well.

1. *Over answering.* Pay close attention to the interviewer's body language—you can usually tell if what you are saying is still relevant. It is a good practice to give the interviewer the chance to choose if you should go into further detail.

2. *Answering with yes or no.* Think of each question an interviewer offers you as a chance to differentiate yourself from the competition and as a chance to show you can add value to their organization. The interviewer is likely to expect something more descriptive—don't short change yourself with a brief answer.

3. *Exaggerating or being dishonest.* Many interviewers ask follow-up questions or record your answers for future interviewers in the organization to see. A lie not only jeopardizes your chances, but also may reflect poorly on your university.

4. *Being a speedy mouth.* It is always more effective to state your thoughts clearly without unnecessary articles like "um" and "like." If you find yourself rambling, take a moment to take a deep breath and think about what you really want to focus on.

5. *Apologizing.* You may be tempted to repeatedly say "I'm sorry" unnecessarily. It is important to be polite, but after a certain extent, it can reflect poorly on your confidence and character.

6. *Saying anything negative.* Some common forms are bad mouthing an old boss or making excuses. Stay positive and find a bright side to an issue regardless of what comes up.

7. *Being too humble.* This is about you—it is not selfish or inappropriate to market yourself during an interview. A common mistake is to down-play accomplishments or talk about successful friends rather than yourself.

Profile
Jeremy Gruenefelder

Who do you work for, what is your official job title, and where is the job located?

I work for Caterpillar Inc. as an Associate Design Engineer in Decatur, Illinois.

Was it your first choice?

Considering that Caterpillar is like a Mechanical Engineer's paradise—yes. I was also considering a position with Boeing which actually was in a better location in my opinion. Decatur is a pretty small town.

What are some positive aspects of the job?

It's a very constructive culture which is perfect for someone starting a career. There isn't much pressure—everyone trusts each other to get the job done. The hours are flexible and during my time working here I've only been presented with a deadline once. The five member hydraulics team I work on is awesome and the modeling work I do in Pro/Engineer is very rewarding. I love my job.

What are some negative aspects?

The only thing I can really think of is the location. I get around it by living in Springfield, but I have to commute an hour everyday.

What is your typical day like?

I get in the office around 7:30 AM. The first half hour consists of checking voice-mail and email. I'm the most productive before lunch so my finest hydraulics design work in Pro/E is done at this time. On average, I have two hours of meetings a day and they usually fall within the morning hours.

I usually have lunch around 11 AM in the cafeteria if I want to make it quick or off-site. Normally, I have lunch with other groups to hear what they are up to. For example, I sometimes have lunch with the light fabrications team, chassis team, or element analysis team.

After lunch I go back to creating digital models. Sometimes I go over to the shop and help the workers that actually build the parts from my designs.

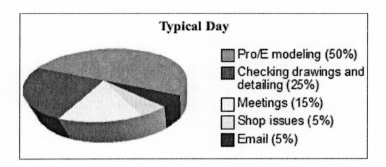

How did you make initial contact with Caterpillar?

I was able to talk to some of their representatives during an on campus job fair. They immediately indicated that they were interested in interviewing me a few days later. I had a campus interview in early April. I didn't hear back for quite some time and had honestly given up all hope, until they contacted me again in early June. I then was invited to a site interview.

How did you prepare for your interviews?

Having completed all my core mechanical engineering coursework, I was confident in my knowledge of the field. So, I focused mainly on company research. I went to the Caterpillar website and learned as much as I could about their product lines. I was able to find out a lot about the Decatur site. I soon found out that they manufacture loader trucks, motor graters, and wheel tractor scrapers there.

What was your site visit like?

I stayed at hotel the night before and was treated to breakfast by a host the next morning. The host was an engineering recent hire which made me feel more comfortable. After breakfast, they brought me on site and gave me three 1-hour interviews. My interviews were 5% HR, 5% technical, and 90% behavioral. After the interviews I had lunch with the host again and was invited to take a tour of the plant. It was a breathtaking site to see the world's largest trucks being built.

Something that may be of interest is the interviewing system that was used. The host actually gave me a lot of encouraging advice including a methodology for answering questions called S.T.A.R. It stands for Situation, Task, Action, and Result. So, when asked behavioral questions, I was encouraged to answer them in this format.

What advice do you have for answering tough behavioral questions?

The most important thing is to relax and be yourself. The interviewer just wants to know if you would make a good teammate. When you aren't sure how you should go about answering a question, lean on the side of conservatism. Innovative answers can work well, but be sure the answer will connect well with the interviewer.

It is always okay to take some time to think! I used to close my eyes and sit back to formulate my answer for a bit. This way, you and your interviewer will have a clear sense of where your answer is going. It's not an exam—it's a conversation.

What would you recommend a candidate do if they can't think of an answer to a question?

Most behavioral questions are very broad. So, you can almost always answer them if you think of previous work experience, coursework, or leadership experience. The answers certainly do not have to be related to engineering or science. Most of my answers for teamwork behavioral questions were about a job I had at Best Buy as a sales associate. My answers had nothing to do with the job I was interviewing for.

If you had to do it all over again, what would you change?

During college I was very focused on graduating early. Looking back, I wish I had sought out more opportunities outside of class such as a co-op. I think I missed out on networking with rising stars my age, having the perspective of working for a different organization, and getting out of class for a semester. I had an offer to do a co-op my sophomore year, but I turned it down because it didn't fit into my four year plan.

789 Crowell Rd., Apt. 01   Phone (217)-556-8173
Carbondale, IL 62902   siu_engr82@hotmail.com

Jeremy A. Gruenenfelder

Objective	To obtain an entry-level engineering position working in research and development.
Education	2000 – 2004 Southern Illinois University Carbondale

B.S. in Mechanical Engineering
- Led a team of student engineers to successfully design vibration damper for applications at $600^\circ C$ and above.
- Specialization in Finite Element Analysis, HVAC, Three Dimensional Modeling, and Compressible Flows.
- Ample experience with AutoDesk Inventor, ANSYS, MATLAB, Microsoft Office, Spreadsheet Design, Working Model and many other common programs using in the engineering profession.

Professional
- State of Illinois, EIT

Interests
- Systems Modeling and Controls.
- Materials Selection.
- Fluids Systems.
- Finite Element Analysis.
- Machine Design.

Awards
- Graduated Cum Laude.
- Participant in Southern Illinois University's Honors Program.
- College of Engineering Dean's List, all semesters.
- Nominated for Top 25 Graduating Seniors.

Engineering GPA = 3.84/4.0   Overall GPA = 3.72/4.0

Work experience   June 2003 to November 2003   Best Buy   Carbondale, IL
Computer Sales Associate

Summer 2002   Illinois Department of Nuclear Safety   Springfield, IL
Calibration Lab Intern

Summer 2001   Dana Brake Parts   Litchfield, IL
Manual Labor

Activities
- Vice President of Tau Beta Pi Illinois Epsilon Chapter.
- Senior Design Project Manager involving the design of a high temperature damper.

9

Technical Interviews

A technical or industry specific interview asks questions related to your field. Technical interviews can also include questions that test your deductive reasoning, critical thinking, and analytical skills. As you will soon learn, success in these supposedly high pressure interviews is primarily dependent on the candidate's approach rather than a high IQ or a photographic memory. This chapter covers the underlying reasoning for technical interviews, provides a detailed inspection of different types of questions you may encounter, and offers some sample questions to practice.

If you have a technical interview coming up, it is recommended that you review *Chapter 8: Behavioral Interviews* as well. Most technical interviews are not purely technical discussions with brain teasers. For example, many technical interviews start with open-ended behavioral questions.

THE PURPOSE BEHIND TECHNICAL INTERVIEWS

Many candidates immediately associate technical questions with intelligence. The assumption made is that employers that use technical interview questions are seeking a prodigy with an unlimited capacity of industry knowledge. This is not necessarily true; what employers really want are people that will add value to their organization. They are looking for someone to get their work done and help their business succeed. If your IQ were a direct indicator of how much value you can bring to employers, job interviews wouldn't exist—people would be hired based on exam scores.

More accurately, technical interviews are designed to determine the following information:

- *Is the candidate a strong problem solver?* Problem solving is what engineers and scientists do on a daily basis. Employers are often looking for someone who enjoys solving problems and embraces a challenge.

- *Does he or she have motivation?* Engineers are not expected to be the type to give up easily. The employer simply wants to make sure you can be relied upon to get the job done. They also want to make sure you are passionate in the type of work they are offering.

- *Is the candidate knowledgeable in his or her field?* The employer wants to make sure you can do the job. The more you know about the tools used and the type of work the position involves, the better you can differentiate yourself.

- *Is he or she a fit for our culture?* Interviewers will often be on the same team as a new hire. Many technical questions evaluate how you would fit in with the group's culture. For example, it may be a hands-on engineering culture, a culture that relies on its employees to innovate in order to create new products, or it may be a high-tech culture.

Technical interviews are discussions just like behavioral interviews. Don't be afraid to share your opinions and insights. Treat it just like a discussion about your field or coursework with a friend. Think out-loud and show the interviewer how you're attacking the problem. A good interviewer will tactfully guide you toward the solution with encouragement.

BRAIN TEASERS

Brain teasers became popular during the dot-com bubble in the late nineties for programming interviews, but now are part of nearly any industry interview including business consulting and law firm interviews. Brain teasers don't involve industry knowledge, but they do test your problem solving skills and motivation. Brain teasers do not utilize any prior knowledge (unless of course you happen to be familiar with the specific puzzle or riddle). It is ironic, because if you find yourself tempted to apply an equation or methodology learned in your coursework, it is a sure sign that you are attacking the problem from the wrong direction.

It is crucial to understand what the real answer to a brain teaser is—which is your approach. The solution to a riddle, puzzle, or game doesn't show the interviewer anything about your problem solving skills or analytical ability, but the journey you take to arrive to that solution does. Thus, it is possible to arrive at the wrong solution to a brain teaser, but still deliver a strong, impressive performance.

Once you know the key to brain teasers is to show strong problem solving skills—instead of trying to win a game for which you barely know the rules—brain teasers become a good opportunity to differentiate yourself against the competition.

How can you show strong problem solving skills? Consider the following techniques:

- *Talk constantly.* The more information the interviewer has about your thinking, the more information they have about your problem solving ability. Talking out-loud also naturally helps you to organize your thoughts.

- *Write constantly.* If you have paper or a white board available, make use of it even if the only thing you do is draw a pictures of what the question asks.

- *Use a structured approach or a plan.* A common mistake is to try and find a solution immediately. Many brain teasers cannot be solves immediately without key information that is missing initially. Try to lay out a plan of how you intend to make your way to the solution. For example, your plan may include different ways you intend to systematically attack the problem. Not only does this give you a road-map, but more importantly, it shows the interviewer where you are going.

- *List your assumptions.* Many brain teasers trick you into making almost sub-conscious assumptions. For example, "There is a cabin on the side of a mountain" could be part of a brain teaser that involves a plane that has crashed. The common assumption made is that the cabin is a log cabin instead of an airplane cabin. Get in the habit of listing your assumptions and questioning their validity.

- *List your resources.* What tools have you been given to solve the problem? It is rare for a detail to be given in a brain teaser that does not have a specific purpose.

A final word of advice for brain teasers in general is not to spend all of your time practicing them. What's important is that you practice a few to become familiar with what is really oral problem solving. It is rare for an interview to have more than one brain teaser. They often serve as an ice breaker at the beginning of a technical interview. Your time is far better spent researching the organization or practicing other types of technical questions rather than memorizing solutions to brain teasers from a database. It is often easy to find out if the employer you are interviewing for asks brain teasers—an online search for accounts of previous interviews is usually sufficient.

The rest of this section covers specific types of brain teasers.

Riddles

A riddle is a question that includes a set of facts that seem unrelated or contradictory, but with the help of missing information, have underlying logical reasoning. Riddles often start at the end of a story that makes little sense. You have to use deductive reasoning to determine how the story began and evolved into the given situation.

Riddles often promote false assumptions. When you encounter a riddle, try to keep a list of every assumption you make. Not only do you have to look out for poor assumptions, but you most likely do not have the entire picture. The good news is that the missing information has to be divulged by the interviewer in some form which is almost always in answers to yes or no questions. In fact, most riddles are nearly impossible without asking good questions. Ask broad questions rather then specific questions. They allow you to narrow down possibilities quickly. Here are some examples of broad questions:

- Is the setting of the situation significant?

- Does the time frame matter?

- Is the entity in question something I could buy at Walmart?

Of course, the context of the riddle determines which broad questions are applicable. To illustrate the process of answering a riddle, consider this example dialog between an interviewer and a candidate based on a riddle asked during a Microsoft interview:

Interviewer: In order to ask the next question, I have to give you some background information first. So, please bear with me.

Candidate: I understand.

Interviewer: Clark is a banker that lives in a 15 story apartment building on the top floor. Every morning, on his way to work, he takes the elevator from the 15th floor to the 1st floor. However, on his way back to his apartment in the afternoons, he takes the elevator from the 1st floor to the 10th floor and then takes 5 flights of stairs.

Why does he bother with five flights of stairs in the afternoons?

Candidate: Is the fact that he is a banker relevant?

Interviewer: No.

Candidate: Is there anything notably different between the elevator Clark uses and the one I used to get to your office this morning?

Interviewer: No.

Candidate: Does the time frame matter? For example, is it significant that he uses the stairs around 5pm?

Interviewer: No.

Candidate: Hmm. Is there anything notable about Clark? Could you or I play the role of Clark in this story?

Interviewer: There is something different about Clark than you or I.

Candidate: *Are his beliefs or values notably different?*

Interviewer: *No.*

Candidate: *Is he physically different?*

Interviewer: *Yes.*

Candidate: *Is he unusually short?*

Interviewer: *Yes.*

Candidate: *I think I have it! Buttons 11 through 15 in the elevator are out of his reach. So, he is forced to use the highest one he can reach in the afternoons which is the button for the 10th floor.*

Interviewer: *Well done.*

Quantitative Brain Teasers

These interview questions seemingly ask the impossible such as "How many gas stations are there in the United State?" It is likely that the interviewer doesn't even care to know what the accurate numerical value is. What is really being tested is your ability to arrive at a number by using logical reasoning. Again, it is a test of your problem solving skills.

Assumptions are crucial for quantitative questions as well, but instead of eliminating assumptions, you must create them. For example, you may need to assume the population of the United States to form a starting point for the gas station question. Keep track of the assumptions you make because the interviewer may question the validity of your answer at the end. The final number is directly dependent on your initial assumptions.

There are two approaches you can take with these problems—a top-down approach or a bottom-up approach. For example, consider the gas station question again. You could start with an estimate of the population for the United States and then make an assumption on the percentage of Americans who own cars, etc. You could also start with the number of times a person fills up their gas tank in a week to determine their consumption over time. Then, you could make an assumption about how many customers a gas station can service in a given period of time, and so on.

Finally, be sure to use simple math. For example, you could round the number of days in a year to 400 to simplify a division calculation. Be sure to communicate your every move as the interviewer is likely to indicate whether his or she approves of your assumptions. Consider the following dialog based on an engineering consulting interview:

Interviewer: How many public phones are in New York City?

Candidate: If you don't mind, I'd like to take a moment to brainstorm my approach to this question on the white board.

Interviewer: Not a problem—take your time.

[A few moments later]

Candidate: Okay, I'm going to take a top down approach based on the area of New York City.

I plan to start by making a list of assumptions allowing me to link the area of the city to the number of public phones per city block. Once we agree on the assumptions, I plan to run the numbers to get an actual result. Finally, I'll inspect the validity of the result and see if any other factors should be considered like public phones in restaurants.

Interviewer: I like your approach.

Candidate: Thanks. The first assumption to consider is the area of New York City. I don't know much about the size of New York City, but I drove through Austin recently which I'll assume is of similar size. It took me twenty minutes to drive through Austin going around 60 miles per hour which makes it roughly 20 miles long. I'll assume New York City is a square with a height and width of 20 miles.

Interviewer: Sounds reasonable to me.

Candidate: The next assumption I need to make is how many blocks there are per area in New York City. I'll assume that each block has a height and width of a quarter mile.

Interviewer: Sure.

Candidate: Finally, I need to make an assumption of how many phone booths there are per block. I would assume that not every block has a public phone booth since many of them are non-commercial areas such as a park or a block with apartment buildings. I'll assume half of the city blocks apply. I think it's common *to have one phone booth at each intersection. However, one phone booth for each corner of a block would yield four phone booths per intersection. I think I'll draw a quick grid to figure this out.*

[A few moments later]

It seems that to get one phone booth on average per intersection, we need one phone booth per city block. I think that's all I need to start my brief quantitative analysis:

City area = 20 x 20 = 400
Number of city blocks = 400 x 4 = 1,600
Number of non-residential city blocks = 1,600/2 = 800
Total public phone booths = 800

Interviewer: *Does that number seem reasonable to you?*

Candidate: *No it doesn't. There are other types of public phones other than phone booths at intersections. As I hinted at while planning my approach, businesses such as restaurants usually have public phones. So, I'm going to add an additional assumption of how many of these businesses are on city blocks. Again, not all city blocks have businesses on them. I'll assume that half of the city blocks apply and, on average, there are three public phones from businesses per block:*

Number of blocks with businesses = 1,600/2 = 800
Number of additional public phones = 800 x 3 = 2,400
Total public phones = 800 + 2,400 = 3,000

Interviewer: *Does that number seem more reasonable?*

Candidate: *To my best knowledge—yes it does.*

Puzzles

These brian teasers involve arranging objects, ordering a sequence of events, or using given resources to achieve some optimal goal.

As in riddles, your assumptions are important to be aware of. Puzzles are often solved after a key false assumption is uncovered or essential missing information is deduced. Unfortunately, it is rare to be able to ask yes or no questions for puzzles as in riddles.

A common situation while solving puzzles is to go from one extreme of making seemingly no progress to another extreme of suddenly knowing the complete solution. When you find yourself tackling one of these problems and it seems like you are not getting any closer to the solution—do not be discouraged. Perhaps you aren't making progress toward the solution to the puzzle, but you are making progress in showcasing your problem solving skills, which is far more important to the interviewer.

Puzzles often have obvious answers which are inefficient, but serve as a basis to evaluate more effective answers. If applicable, it can be effective to take the less efficient solution and determine why it is not the best approach. The following dialog is based on the technical interviewing performance of one of the contributors to this book:

> **Interviewer:** *Imagine you have a balance that compares the weight placed on two surfaces. You have eight marbles that all weigh the same except for one that weighs less. How can you determine the "odd" marble by using the balance only twice?*

> **Candidate:** *I think I'll begin by studying the obvious, but inefficient, solution of weighing four marbles on each side.*

> **Interviewer:** *Okay.*

> [Candidate draws a balance on the white board similar to Figure 9-1]

Figure 9-1. Balance (odd marble weighs less)

Candidate: *The first use eliminates four marbles and the second eliminates two more. So, this approach requires three uses of the balance. Hmm. No matter how I rearrange the marbles, the balance has two possible outcomes—either the left side is heavier or the right side is.*

Interviewer: *Are you sure the balance only has two states?*

Candidate: *Ahh, it seems I made an assumption. There is a third potential case where the balance is even if both sides weigh the same. In order for that to be possible, only standard marbles would need to be on the balance. So, if I put some marbles on the side, it is possible for the scale to be even.*

Interviewer: *How can you take advantage of that?*

Candidate: *The answer just came to me when I thought of putting marbles on the side. You weigh a total of six marbles on the balance instead of 8, leaving 2 off the balance. If the odd marble happens to be on the balance, you immediately know because the balance is uneven—eliminating all but 3 marbles. If it is the case that the balance is even, you know it is one of the 2 marbles on the side.*

On the second round, if you are down to 2 marbles, you just put one on each side and you're done. If you are down to 3 marbles, you set 2 on the balance and 1 on the side. Whether the balance is uneven or even indicates which of the 3 is the odd marble.

Interviewer: *Nice work.*

TECHNICAL CASE QUESTIONS

A close cousin to brain teasers is a technical case. The main difference is that the solution is open-ended and some of them require industry knowledge. They are another form of testing your analytical and problem solving skills. You are given a hypothetical situation that is more realistic than an abstract brain teaser question, but usually has been simplified due to time constraints.

Another difference is that technical cases are expected to be discussions. You are likely to exchange information with the interviewer throughout the conversation. Technical cases are often modeled from real-world problems.

Be sure you understand the requirements for the problem. The interviewer may purposefully leave you to find out critical details. This can lead to false assumptions and a solution that is completely different than what the interviewer is expecting. For example, "Design a house on the white board" could lead to a very poor performance if the candidate does not ask who the inhabitants will be or what materials are available. Instead, it is always a good idea to make sure you have all the information you need. If you aren't sure you have enough information, restate the facts back to the interviewer or simply ask about your concerns.

Design Problems

A subset of technical cases are design questions. It is usually the design of something related to your field at a high level. Some fundamental knowledge of your field may be required. Sometimes they are closer to a brain teaser where you are designing something abstract. Either way, you are being tested on your skills in architecting a solution to a fairly open-ended problem.

Developing a plan or a structured approach before beginning can be very beneficial for design problems. Consider the following example which requires some knowledge of computer systems based on a real interview question asked during an IBM Extreme Blue interview:

> *Interviewer: How would you design an electronic coupon system for supermarkets?*
>
> *Candidate: Well, the first thing I would do is try to figure out what value this system is to provide. An obvious thing would be to attract new customers, but*

considering how much the typical consumer is saturated with coupons these days, I would think this isn't of huge value.

However, one real value I can see is being able to track what consumers are purchasing. An interesting emerging marketing tool is tracking shopping trends of customers. The most common realization of this is those little discount cards supermarkets already use.

So, the most important thing to me in designing this system is to be able to uniquely mark each coupon (perhaps on a per-user basis) and also to be able to track where the coupon is used.

Interviewer: *Ok, continue with that value proposition.*

Candidate: *Another thing to consider is the source of coupons. Not knowing that much about the shopping industry, I know there's at least two types of coupons—manufacturer's coupons and then store coupons.*

We could support both if we offered some sort of centralized coupon generation system (or perhaps relied on a standards based mechanism to exchange customer data). It's a pretty standard software system though, a centralized database somewhere, the client software at each of the supermarkets, and the ability to upload the data to that centralized place.

So, if we know what the typical supermarket IT infrastructure looks like, we can design the client software. We can then help design the server software based on whatever the central IT infrastructure is for the supermarket chain. To recommend the best platform to use, for example vendor technology or open-source software, I would need to ask more about the supermarket's IT environment.

Interviewer: *I'm afraid we are out of time; however, I like your approach. You focused on the root of the problem to be solved instead of going through a laundry list of technical jargon without analyzing the problem first like most people do. Good job!*

Quality Assurance

Many engineering and computer science positions involve quality assurance or testing. Thus, technical cases often involve finding an error in a process or testing the quality of a hypothetical product.

If the position you are interviewing for has "test engineer" in the title or mentions quality assurance in the description, you may be asked quality assurance technical cases. For example, you could be asked to come up with a plan to test a simplified version of a product when there are not enough resources to cover all possible test cases.

Many quality assurance problems are seemingly trivial such as "How would you test a paper cup?" It may surprise you that it is possible to talk about how to test a paper cup for hours. You could test the paper cup for different user bases, safety, functionality, durability—the list goes on and on. If you think quality assurance may be a key factor in your interview, the following fundamental testing practices should prove helpful:

- *Performance.* Performance testing determines if a product meets the requirements to complete a task within a required time or quantifiable quality of service. For example, measuring the clarity of sound for a speaker is a performance test.

- *Availability.* Availability testing ensures that the product is fully functional for customers within a certain percentage, for example, 99.8% of the time or available to 78% of the user base. It is often too costly for a business to attempt 100% availability. Measuring the percentage of the population in a city that has access to a radio station is a test of availability.

- *Scalability.* Scalability testing inspects the product's ability to scale as more customers use it. For example, testing a telephone network for a million simultaneous users is a scalability test.

- *Security.* Security testing ensures the product protects the producer's and customer's assets such as proprietary or personal information. Testing a website's "permissions" to ensure a customer's personal information cannot be accessed outside of an authorized group, is a basic form of security testing.

- *Usability.* Usability testing inspects the product's quality in the hands of a customer. It ensures the product meets the needs of its users. Holding a focus group where customers cook with a newly developed microwave is an example of usability testing.

- *Safety.* Safety testing makes sure no one can be harmed by the product. For example, testing common scenarios for possible harm to the user—such as accidentally dropping a product or performing maintenance—is a form of safety testing.

- *Stress.* Sometimes called fault-injection, stress testing evaluates the product's robustness and durability under harsh circumstances. Stress testing sometimes involves purposefully taking extremes to see what part of the product fails first or testing the product functionality with missing components. Running a photo-copy machine continuously for weeks is an example of stress testing.

- *Integration.* Integration testing ensures that there are no defects when combining components of a product or when interfacing it with a greater framework or system. For example, when assembling a bicycle, measuring the strength of a connection between the front wheel and the frame can be considered integration testing.

- *Functional.* Functional testing or "black box" testing inspects the inputs and outputs to a system. Ideally, all possible inputs should be tested, but this usually proves to be too expensive in practice. Testing every possible combination of buttons on a TV remote is a form of functional testing.

The purpose of this list is to show that you can attack a quality assurance problem from multiple angles. You don't want to be the candidate that suggestions only one method of testing—making the conversation with the interviewer prematurely brief. On the other hand, don't assume you need to bring up ten testing strategies to an interviewer. What's important is that you talk the entire time and show that you have an effective testing approach.

The list above is not a magic list of testing criteria and should not be memorized. It is not the best list for all situations and certainly not a complete list. Consider constructing a smaller list of criteria that best fits the industry or job description. You can put the list in your briefcase or interviewing folder to serve as possible talking points if you do get asked a testing question.

The following dialog serves as an example based on an interview performance by one of the contributors to this book:

> **Interviewer:** *How would you test a toaster for people who are blind?*

> **Candidate:** *I think ease of use is important for someone who is blind, otherwise the product may not be practical for them. Something else that comes to mind is that if they are alone while using the toaster, it should be made such that they*

cannot get hurt in the event of an accident. So, I think the most important things to test are usability and safety.

[Candidate writes the words 'Usability' and 'Safety' on the white board]

Candidate: *For usability, I would recommend getting some blind volunteers into the lab to get their opinions on the product. Some criteria that comes to mind is testing how well they find the toaster, testing the placement of different types of bread into the toaster, testing how they can determine if the bread is ready, and testing the removal of the bread. I would recommend recording their opinions regarding conventional toasters and any competing products as well.*

That covers my thoughts on usability. If you don't mind, I'd like to move on to safety.

Interviewer: *By all means.*

Candidate: *I think getting volunteers into the lab can help a great deal with safety as well, but there needs to be additional testing so it is nearly impossible for the user to be harmed. A critical test would be to see if there is any way a hot coil can be accidentally touched by a user's hand. Testing the toaster's behavior if it is accidentally dropped and inspecting it for sharp edges also comes to mind.*

Interviewer: *You've described usability and safety quite well, but is there anything else that should be tested?*

Candidate: *So far, I've described testing that would be different from the quality assurance of a conventional toaster. Considerations for any toaster would be stress testing to see how it holds up to frequent use, black box testing to make sure the buttons and knobs function as expected, and performance testing regarding its ability to heat efficiently.*

Interviewer: *Well done. Let's move on to the next question.*

Knowledge-based Questions

Knowledge-based questions range from technical discussions to questions with short answers. What they have in common is that they require deep skills from your field or industry knowledge.

Knowledge-based questions often involve a serious of related questions that build on each other. For example, an interviewer may ask you if you are familiar with an industry tool, then ask you how that tool is used in practice, and finally ask you how you would solve a problem using that tool.

As advised for other types of technical questions, always keep your communication level up with the interviewer by thinking out-loud. What often distinguishes a star candidate from an average interviewee is the insightful information they give in addition to the direct answer to a knowledge-based question. For example, image that "What is CMOS?" is asked during an interview for an electrical engineer. An average candidate may answer with:

> *I think it stands for Complementary Metal Oxide Semiconductor. It's a class of modern integrated circuits.*

A star candidate sees this as an open-ended question and answers with:

> *CMOS is the most widely used integrated circuit design today. Its predecessors were bipolar transistors which use more power. Because of their efficient power consumption, CMOS integrated circuits allow for more computing power per chip. When CMOS circuits became* available *outside the research lab in the early 90's, they helped facilitate the explosion of more powerful and efficient high-end computers which simply are not possible with bipolar transistor technology. I would argue that it contributed to the emergence of the information age.*

It doesn't take an electrical engineer to see that the star candidate shows a strong perspective for his or her field. What is important to note is that the strength of the answer does not lie in the text book definition of CMOS. It lies in the related information the candidate added that wasn't directly asked in the question. The candidates opinions, information on why CMOS was successful, its history, and why it is important were not asked by the interviewer, but the candidate knew to add these things to show a strong industry perspective.

The answers above are ideal examples, because in both cases the candidates know the answer to the question. What if you get stuck or aren't sure of the answer? If you get stuck don't be afraid to tell the interviewer what is on your mind. State what you do know and state the possibilities you are considering. For some questions, it may helpful to systematically attempt to apply different fundamentals from your field. For example, a civil engineer who gets stuck during a discussion related to his or her field may think out-loud as follows:

Well, let's see if I can apply some fundamentals to this problem. Does statics or physics apply? Can dynamics play a role in this problem? Does the strength of the materials matter? Can my knowledge of fluid mechanics help?

Programming Questions

It is undeniable that computer engineers and computer scientists have some of the most rigorous technical interviews. A subset of questions that require industry specific knowledge are programming questions which certainly deserve special attention.

Programming questions often have an inefficient, slow, or memory intensive solution that first comes to mind. This is almost invariably the place to start. Be sure to explain that you realize it is not the most elegant or efficient solution, but it will serve as your starting point.

Expect to get stuck in programming problems. This is a very critical part of the process of answering programming questions (or any technical question for that matter), because your character is tested when faced with the unknown. Above all else, do not give up! You've gone through countless nights of unrelenting course-work and studying—this is no time to be a wimp.

When you are stuck, a good approach is to collect more information by going over simple examples. As much as you want to give the interviewer an elegant solution by purely thinking abstractly, doing simple tests of an algorithm or approach can be very insightful. For example, you may want to test how you would solve a problem using one or two elements instead of in the general case.

Everyone has their own style for writing code, but if you are tempted, fight the urge to begin writing code immediately with the hopes to solve the problem along the way. Talk to the interviewer and solve the problem at a high level first. One approach is to write comments on a white board which dictate what the code will do. When you are satisfied with the comments, erase them and replace them with real code (if you have space you can leave the comments in). This is an excellent technique because if you run out of time, the interviewer knows your approach is correct and would result in the correct solution. Consider the following example of a list of comments for removing an element from a linked list:

Check to make sure the linked list is not empty

Create and initialize references for the current Element (head) and the next Element

Check and handle the special case of a linked list with a single element

Create a loop which iterates through the linked list

If next Element refers to the node to be removed:

Remove by overwriting next Element reference

Free the unlinked element from memory

Exit loop

The above example has very specific comments which mostly correspond to a single line of code. Depending on your programming style and your familiarity with the topic, feel free to use higher level comments such as "Iterate through loop and remove node" which would correspond to several lines of code.

In a top-down approach as described above, making the transition from comments to pseudo code should be fairly trivial—the hard work is getting the comments correct. Very few candidates could write out the comments to the above problem immediately without errors. So, expect to erase, shuffle, and rewrite them as you orally brainstorm with your interviewer. That is part of why this approach is recommended—shuffling around sentence fragments should prove to be a lot easier than rewriting actual code.

There are various things you can to do prepare for programming questions. Consider the following strategies:

- *Practice, practice, practice.* When you practice, talk out-loud so you can get used to forming your thoughts orally. Getting the answers to the problems is not as important as fine-tuning your approach.

- *Review the fundamentals from your coursework.* Pay special attention to algorithms, data structures, and complexity analysis (Linear time, Big-O of n^2, and so forth).

- *Practice programming problems involving technologies listed on your resume.* Reviewing by example allows you to practice your technique for programming questions and also helps prevent embarrassing situations where you are unfamiliar with a technology listed on your resume. Of course, if company research or the job description points you toward a specific type of development, try to find problems to practice related to that discipline as well.

- *Get used to pseudo code.* When you are practicing, try to be consistent in the pseudo code you use. Reflect on your solutions—find ways to do things in short-hand. Practice and improve your pseudo code until it is second nature.

- *Talk about your programming best practices.* In most cases, you will only have time to write out a simple solution to a problem. When discussing a solution, it is crucial to explain how you would solve the problem in a real development environment. For example, discussions on proper initialization, abstraction, encapsulation, singular return, strong typing, proper object lifecycle management, error handling, the tools you would use, and design patterns always distinguishes candidates. Of course, what you discuss depends on your style of programming and what you believe in, but having an opinion is often considered favorable.

Quick Ways to Sharpen Your Technical Interviewing Technique

The following techniques should prove useful in any technical interview. Many of them have been touched on before, but deserve to be re-emphasized:

- *Think out-loud.* Keep talking to show the interviewer how you think.

- *Show the interviewer where you are going.* It is ok to take a moment and explain how you are going to approach the problem. If you just start rambling from the beginning you could end up with a laundry list of unrelated ideas which do not market you as a strong problem solver.

- *Welcome the challenge.* A strong candidate is not discouraged when they are at a loss of where to start. Try to find interest in the problem presented. Pull out your curious side and be enthusiastic.

- *Have an opinion.* During technical discussions, it is often beneficial to state your opinions on the topic at hand. With the religious wars that revolve around technology, industry tools, and competing products—not having an opinion about things is like being a politician without a message. Of course, be sure you can defend your opinion with related facts or past experiences.

- *Always look like you are thinking.* Even if you have a complete memory lapse, stay calm, look studious, and try to show a constructive approach. As a similar saying goes—it is better to look like you are motivated and engaged on solving a problem than to remove all doubt.

- *If you are a senior or grad student, review fundamental coursework.* It can be embarrassing to forget basic concepts from your field or how a previous project worked. You shouldn't spend hours on it, but brushing up on subjects you haven't worked with in years can improve your confidence and may prove useful.

- *Brainstorm for a few seconds before you answer a question.* Solutions to technical questions benefit a great deal from a general plan laid out at the beginning even if it's something like "I plan to draw a picture on the white board, list different ways of attacking the problem, and to end with a final recommendation." A little structure can go a long way in showing your interviewer that you are a strong problem solver.

- *Add realistic observations wherever possible.* Most technical interview questions are simplified or abstract which can give you an opportunity to make comparisons to how such problems are solved in the real world. This can be a good way to show you have an industry perspective.

- *Practice with a real white board.* Unless you often teach, writing on a white board is probably not very natural. If you have access to a classroom or office with a white board try to do all your practice questions on it. Familiarity can go a long way to reduce nervousness and can improve the quality of what you write during an interview.

SAMPLE QUESTIONS

The following sample questions, divided by discipline where applicable, should serve as some good practice. Even thought many of them were recently asked in real technical interviews, it is not likely that you will be asked the same questions. In fact, focusing on the solutions is of little value at all. *Your goal should be to master your approach and interviewing technique* rather than concentrating on a particular solution to a problem. The solutions by number are provided later in this chapter. It is strongly recommended that you use these questions for mock interviews. The following section, "Online Resources for Questions," lists sources for additional sample questions.

Brain Teasers

1. There are three light bulbs in another room which you cannot see into. You have three switches in front of you that correspond to the light bulbs. The switches map to the light bulbs in a random order. You have permission to visit the room with the light bulbs once. How can you determine which switch corresponds to each light bulb?

2. Ann is upstairs reading in a two story house. It's getting late, so she turns out the light and goes downstairs to sleep. Later that night, several men—apparently airborne—hit the side of her house in wet tattered clothes. Many of them are mortally injured. This is Ann's fault. Why?

3. How many bottles of sample size shampoo are manufactured every year?

4. Claire and Frank are brother and sister. When you arrive on the scene, they are lying on the ground motionless in the living room of a house with broken glass and water everywhere. What happened?

5. Using only a five-gallon bucket and a three-gallon bucket, measure exactly four-gallons of water in the five-gallon bucket.

6. A king has recently found out that a single bottle from his wine collection was poisoned. It is a rare form of poison that does not show signs of infection for a month. The king has ten prisoners sentenced to death in his dungeon at his disposal. How can he determine which bottle of wine was poisoned in one month?

Quality Assurance

7. How would you test a stapler?

8. Test an elevator that will be installed in a hospital. You do not have access to the hospital.

Aeronautical Engineering

9. If a prototype plane does not take off, how can you determine the problem?

10. How can you be certain an aircraft will not fall apart during flight?

Chemical Engineering

11. Design a system to remove caffeine from coffee beans.

12. Why does gasoline explode?

Civil Engineering

13. Design a modern road.

14. What are pumps in series and pumps in parallel?

Computer Engineering

15. What is pipelining?

16. What is the difference between an analog and digital circuit?

17. Design a 1-bit full adder. Your resources are two OR gates and a decoder.

18. What do you know about caching schemes?

Computer Science

19. How would you reverse a linked list?

20. Given a lengthy ransom note that you'd like to build and the letters in a magazine as input, write a program that determines if the magazine has enough characters in it to assemble the ransom note.

21. Imagine you have a jigsaw puzzle to assemble. You have a function that takes in two puzzle piece sides and returns true only if the two sides interlock perfectly. The function returns true only once for each possible combination of sides. You also know whether a side of a piece sticks out, curves inward, is a piece along the outer border, and whether a given piece is a corner piece. Additionally, you are given the bottom-left corner piece to start with. How would you solve the puzzle?

22. Print a complete binary tree by level starting with the root.

Electrical Engineering

23. What is a transistor?

24. For CMOS logic, give the various techniques you know to minimize power consumption.

25. Describe the different types of filters you know.

26. What are P-type and N-type configurations?

Industrial and Systems Engineering

27. What is you familiarity with throughput, inventory and operating expenses?

28. How would you design an assembly line balancing procedure?

Materials Science and Mechanical Engineering

29. What are the three different modes of heat transfer?

30. What is the difference between static failure and fatigue failure?

ONLINE RESOURCES FOR QUESTIONS

Brain Teasers

- http://www.greylabyrinth.com—*The Grey Labyrinth*

- http://www.ocf.berkeley.edu/~wwu/riddles—*...:: Riddles ::... by William Wu*

- http://www.techinterview.org—*techInterview*

Other

- http://www.techinterviews.com/?p=101—*Tech Interviews:* Excellent collection of question for technology related fields. To illustrate its usefulness, the link provided here is for questions asked during interviews at Intel.

- http://www.vault.com—*VAULT:* Includes interview guides with questions for selected fields and active forums containing first hand interviewing experiences.

- http://www.eng-tips.com—*ENG-TIPS FORUMS:* Provides forums with some reported interviewing experiences.

- http://www.sellsbrothers.com/fun/msiview—*Microsoft Interview Questions:* A collection of interviewing questions from Microsoft Corporation.

ANSWERS TO SAMPLE QUESTIONS

While conducting mock interviews, these solutions can serve as a guide to the mock interviewer. It is important to note that these are sample solutions and are by no means the best solutions to the given questions. A strong solution often depends on the discussion you have with an interviewer and where they steer the conversation.

This section is designed to provide hints before the entire solution. The solutions given here are far more verbose than what would be expected in an interview. The solutions are more complete in order to show what the potential is for a solution. A strong solution is likely to contain only a small subset of the information provided for each question (or other insights not considered here).

(1)
Type: Puzzle

Hint: Leaving a switch in the "ON" position for an extended period of time is useful.

Hint: Heat plays a part in the solution.

Solution: Assuming the switches are labeled A, B, and C—turn switch A on for 20 minutes. Then, turn switch A off and turn switch B on. Walk to the room with the light bulbs. The bulb that is off, but warm, corresponds to switch A. The bulb that is on corresponds to switch B and the remaining bulb corresponds to switch C.

Follow-up question: What if one of the bulbs in faulty?

Follow-up solution: Possible solutions involve pulling out the wiring for the bulbs to see if the wires spark when touched to test for current and leaving two bulbs on for different amounts of time so one is very hot and the other is warm when inspected.

(2)
Type: Riddle (Yes/No questions are allowed)

Hint: "It's getting late so she turns out the light" is significant.

Hint: Ann does not live in a typical house and it is on the beach.

Solution: Ann lives in a lighthouse. Ann made the mistake of turning off the guiding light. The men are sailors and their ship collided with the lighthouse.

(3)
Type: Quantitative brain teaser

Hint: Be sure to ask your interviewer for necessary details such as whether the question implies sample bottles produced worldwide or in the US and whether sample size conditioner should be included. In this case, assume only sample shampoo bottles manufactured worldwide are considered. You can assume sample size shampoo is manufactured for two purposes—hotels and promotions.

Hint: It is best to focus on the number of hotels in the world first and then add promotions as a percentage of hotel use.

Solution: A top-down approach is to estimate the number of hotels in the world and their demand for sample bottles. Hotels usually center around major metropolitan areas. Start by estimating the number of countries in the world and how many cities a country has on average. Then you can make an assumption of how many hotels are in each city. Once you have the number of hotels, estimate how many occupied rooms hotels have on average. You may want to consider that a percentage of guests do not use or take home the complementary bottles. Scale your estimate of bottles used in a day to a year.

You can estimate how many promotional shampoo bottles are produced yearly starting with city population or simply by adding a small percentage to the amount manufactured for hotels. Your final solution should be in the multi-millions range not exceeding a billion.

(4)
Type: Riddle

Hint: The amount of glass and water is relatively small—perhaps a gallon of water and enough glass to cover a small coffee table.

Hint: Claire and Frank are not human.

Solution: Claire and Frank are fish. Their fish tank got knocked over.

(5)
Type: Puzzle

Hint: Measuring two gallons of water is not part of the solution.

Hint: Try creating a single gallon of water first.

Solution: Fill the three-gallon bucket and pour it into the five-gallon bucket. Fill the three gallon bucket again and pour it into the five-gallon bucket until it is full to measure one gallon. Empty the five-gallon bucket and pour in the single gallon. Fill the three-gallon bucket again, pour it into the five-gallon bucket, and you have exactly four gallons.

(6)
Type: Puzzle (Yes/No questions may be allowed)

Hint: The poison is so potent that even a drop has the same effect and the king does not mind using a small amount of wine from each bottle for testing purposes.

Hint: Think of the 10 prisoners as a key which is somehow unique for each bottle of wine.

Solution: Line up the prisoners and number the prisoners from 0-9. Assign each bottle of wine a code which assigns which prisons should drink from it. For example, the code for one of the wine bottles may be TTTTTFFFFF where the first five prisoners drink the bottle, but the remaining ones do not.

At the end of the month, the prisoner(s) left uninfected will match the code of the poisoned bottle. There are 2^{10} possible permutations or 1024 which is more than enough to cover the 1000 bottles. If you are a programmer or electrical engineer it would prove impressive to use 1's and 0's as this is nothing more than binary encoding.

(7)
Type: Quality assurance

Hint: Consider the ways a stapler can fail to function and develop tests for such cases.

Hint: Try to apply the fundamentals in the quality assurance section.

Solution: A necessarily brief solution follows:

- *Performance testing.* Performance may be tested by timing the creation of a single staple, switching to "tacking mode," and timing reloading of staples.

- *Usability and safety testing.* These can be tested by having volunteers continuously create staples for an extended period of time. For example, repeated use may result in a soar thumb which would reflect poorly usability or a staple may injure one of the volunteers indicating a safety problem.

- *Integration testing.* A check that all the components are properly installed such as the anvil, magazine tension spring, pivot spring, body, and base can facilitate integration testing. Additionally, testing that all the components are securely in place by applying pressure at different points is a form of integration testing.

- *Functional testing.* Testing the stapler on different types of paper both in regular and tacking mode can serve as a functional test.

- *Stress testing.* Forms of stress testing are attempting to staple increasingly thicker stacks of paper, systematically testing to see if the stapler functions with missing components such as a screw, and continuously stapling and reloading until the device no longer functions.

(8)
Type: Quality assurance

Hint: Think about what types of testing are made more difficult because there is no access to the hospital.

Hint: Just because you don't have access to a hospital, doesn't mean you cannot mimic the environment.

Solution: One approach is to assume the manufacturer often tests elevators, but does not have experience in designing an elevator for a hospital. Thus, the solution can be divided into two parts—hospital elevator specific testing and testing for elevators in general. The following tests fall under quality assurance unique to hospital elevators:

- *Scalability testing.* Getting the specifications for the standard size of hospital beds may prove useful in testing how many patients accompanied by nurses can fit in the elevator.

- *Safety testing.* This is likely to be the most significant consideration for the interviewer. Each material of the elevator should be inspected for possible allergic reactions and maintainability of sanitation. Testing the safety of the doors should be done to ensure it is impossible for them to close on a slow moving, frail patient. Test the elevator's environment to be sure nothing promotes injury such as a sharp edge or a piece of molding that can be caught by a hospital gown.

- *Usability testing.* This can be done by simulating the needs of a hospital on a typical day. For example, usability may be tested with the elderly or with some modern wheelchairs. Some things to consider are the usefulness of the buttons, the usefulness of the elevator in the event that it is stuck, and the usefulness of any railings or hand rests.

If time allows, the following testing are appropriate for elevators in general:

- *Performance testing.* This includes measuring how fast the elevator transports its cargo between varying displacement of floors and measuring how much weight it can hold.

- *Availability testing.* A form of availability testing is measuring the elevator's responsiveness after selecting the button to call it from a floor.

- *Stress testing.* This includes applying increasingly stronger pressure on it's components to analyze structural integrity, testing it's functionality when proper maintenance is neglected, and testing to see if it works with various missing or improperly installed components.

- *Functional testing.* Forms of functional testing include testing key combinations of its buttons and testing that it can reach the amount of floors in its specifications.

(9)

Type: Knowledge-based

Hint: Think about why things you may use on a daily basis can fail to function properly such as a car or a toaster.

Hint: Think about the engineering courses you have taken, nearly every one should apply.

Solution: It is very important to emphasize how you would solve the problem or how you would design the plane differently to prevent possible faults. This is an open-ended question, so your solution should involve concepts which you are most familiar with, what you are passionate about, and your industry perspective. However, here are some considerations:

- *Problems with the pilot.* Explaining that human error is a very common cause of flight problems may show your interviewer that you think objectively.

- *Take-off distance.* Without a long enough runway, the plane cannot achieve the proper air pressure for take-off. Many airports and plane specifications define standard take-off distances (TOD). A comparison to the TOD of a similar plane may be beneficial.

- *Lift.* Without the proper amount of force due to dynamic pressure of airflow the plane cannot take-off. The study of aerodynamics tells us that factors such as the shape of the wing, the density of the air, the velocity of the air, the wing's surface area, and the wing-span can affect lift.

- *Drag.* Wind and weather can be a consideration for the flight of an experimental prototype. L/D ratios representing life over drag are often used in industry. Many planes have a documented L/D ratio in their specifications for a safe takeoff. L/D ratios can also be tested in wind tunnels.

- *Thrust.* The thrust provided by the engine(s) is a significant factor. An engine may not be producing enough thrust to produce lift. Static thrust tests are often done on engines where they are tested in place to ensure the fuel system and engine is fully functional. Any observations you have from your coursework regarding thrust should be mentioned such as power-weight ratios, torque associated with propellers, energy, inertia, etc.

- *Weight.* The force due to gravity is dependent on weight. Additional weight requires more energy created by the airflow over the wings to produce lift. Related to L/D ratios, thrust over weight ratios (T/W) are also often studied. Making a plane lighter can be a remedy to an experimental plane that cannot take off.

(10)
Type: Quality assurance

Hint: Think about what can cause structural instability.

Hint: Integration testing and stress testing are of paramount concern for this question.

Solution: Consider the following tests:

- *Functional testing.* Testing that all the components on the plane are present and meet the original specifications of its design could prevent failing parts or detect maintenance requirements.

- *Stress testing.* The materials used in the aircraft should be tested to ensure they can sustain the strain of flight. Some examples would be to test beams for lateral-torsional buckling and to test plated structures for buckling under axial loads or shearing.

- *Integration testing.* Even if the individual components based on adequate materials provide stability, the joints or interconnections of these components may not. Assuming that the current plane has undergone sufficient maintenance, the interconnection of components can be tested by simulation. Either by using real models or software models (such as MIDAS/Gen), the structure can be analyzed for failure points and vulnerable integration. Coursework related to structural stability such as Statics would prove useful in your discussion with the interviewer.

- *Vibration testing.* A special case for this situation is testing the frequency of the plane during flight. The plane creates a certain frequency during flight affected by wind, jittery actuators, very flexible structures, etc. If a plane's second mode of vibration is reached, the resonance can cause major structural damage. This can be tested with frequency instruments in a wind tunnel or during test flights.

(11)
Type: Design problem

Hint: The coffee beans still need to taste like coffee after decaffeination.

Hint: Think about how substances can be filtered or dissolved in general.

Solution: This is not an easy question; the interviewer would certainly provide guidance to spark a healthy discussion. A constructive approach would be to talk about how other chemicals are separated, purified, or filtered. In the coffee industry, there are three popular forms of decaffeination—by solvent, water extraction, and CO_2 extraction:

Solvents dissolve caffeine and are moderately to slightly toxic in most cases. For example, earlier forms of solvents were benzene and chloroform. The solvent of choice more recently (until the early 90's) was ethyl acetate which is in many common fruits. It is proven to be slightly toxic, but was marketed as "natural" because of its presence in fruit. This method is rarely used today.

Water extraction uses hot water for about eight hours to extract about 98% of the caffeine from green coffee beans. The resulting coffee beans contain little caffeine, but also contain little flavor as well. The commonly used solution is to filter the extracted water which contains the coffee flavor with activated charcoal. The coffee beans are then soaked in the filtered extract until the flavor returns.

CO_2 extraction exploits special properties of supercritical fluids. A supercritical fluid, which shares properties of both gases and liquids, can be created under high temperature and pressure. Supercritical CO_2 is created and put through green coffee beans. In this form it is an effective solvent which is non-polar. Its gas-like properties allow it to flow through nearly all the coffee bean matter.

(12)
Type: Knowledge-based

Hint: Explosions usually result from rapidly moving molecules or atoms.

Hint: Breaking chemical bonds releases energy.

Solution: According to the second law of thermodynamics energy disperses whenever possible. This is known as entropy. In the case of a mixture of gasoline and oxygen, they both have a lot of stored energy in their chemical bonds. They desperately want to release this energy by forming carbon dioxide and water. However, a small amount of energy is needed to make this transition such as a spark. The chemical reaction that creates the first carbon dioxide and water molecules releases a relatively large amount of energy which allows for more chemical bonds to be broken creating a chain reaction. Tremendous heat and pressure results.

(13)
Type: Design problem

Hint: The question is deceivingly brief—your first instincts should be to validate initial assumptions. The information to find out from the interviewer is what the road is being built for, whether it is public or private, what locations it will connect, and whether there are any terrain or geographical considerations like mountains or lakes. For this case, assume you are designing a three-lane public highway which spans 100 miles through flat countryside. It's being built to connect two other main routes, but concentrate on the majority of the road rather than the endpoints.

Hint: In additional to materials and structural standards—the weather, planning the route, and the existing landscape are considerations.

Solution: This question is designed to spark a civil engineering discussion. Designing a road takes years, so there is a wealth of potential for you to create a constructive exchange. A strong approach is to brainstorm a diverse list of considerations such as—the route planning, pavement, hydrology and erosion, landscape architecture, and legal standards. This list is not complete, in any particular order, or even required to provide a strong solution.

In a real interview a star candidate would think about the qualities of a successful highway (mostly from his or her own experiences driving on them) and come up with a few good talking points. For completeness, here are some brief descriptions of the list given above:

- *Route planning.* "Sight distance" or the amount of highway a driver can see ahead and behind is usually a consideration for route planning. Thus, there should not be sharp turns, steep hills, or structures that may block a driver's vision. Additionally, costly terrain related concerns such as bridges and tunnels should be avoided if possible.

- *Pavement.* It is desirable (and often required by law) to build a road that is horizontally aligned and flat. For example, a slight "U" shaped contour should be avoided. A modern road usually includes a pavement layer, base layer, and sub-base layer constructed from various types of asphalt.

- *Hydrology and erosion.* Runoff of water is the key to this consideration. Peak discharge or peak flow is usually analyzed to find the maximum flow of water over the road during rainfall (it would be wise to ask the interviewer if the area often floods). A drainage basin is usually carefully designed for major highways. Finally, erosion is a very real concern—a study of the terrain's history and the soil in the area should be conducted.

- *Landscape architecture.* When the base soil is poor, the terrain is not level, or natural obsticals present themselves, the landscape needs to be modified. Even when conditions are desirable, highway construction often mandates the addition of vegetation and irrigation to mitigate environmental concerns. Highways often have medians as well, which need to be properly maintained and designed with safety in mind. Medians also provide space for future construction, accidents, and maintenance which, in effect, reduces lane closures.

(14)
Type: Knowledge-based

Hint: This question falls under the study of hydraulics.

Hint: Both methods have trade-offs.

Solution: Identical hydraulic pumps configured in series are setup such that the output of the first pump is directly connected to the input of the next. The continuity which bounds the maximum speed of the liquid, or "flow rate," being pumped does not increase with the addition of more pumps in a series configuration. However, the total energy capacity of pumps in series does increase with the addition of more pumps. For example, if additional pressure is needed to transport an especially viscous fluid, additional pumps in series can increase the overall pressure of the system.

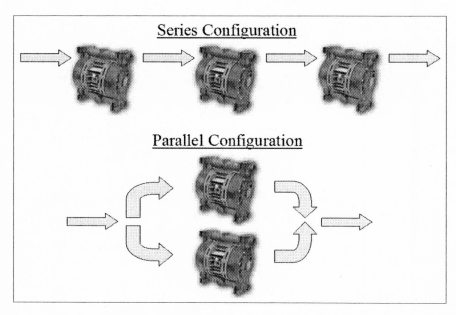

Figure 9-2. Hydraulic pumps in series and in parallel

In a parallel configuration, the fluid is routed to the input to every pump at the same time ("in-parallel"). Identical pumps in parallel are the complete opposite—the continuity scales but the total energy stays the same as a single pump. Thus, the flow rate increases with the addition of a pump, but the total pressure stays the same.

(15)
Type: Knowledge-based

Hint: This question refers to pipelining in a microprocessor.

Hint: It is called pipelining because it is similar in many respects to manufacturing assembly lines where more then one product is assembled at the same time.

Solution: Pipelining is used by most modern CPU's. Machine instructions—such as integer, floating point, and logical operations—can be executed in parallel in a microprocessor pipeline. This is achieved by dividing the processing into pipeline stages where a new instruction is added to the first stage of the pipeline after the previous has finished using it.

The effectiveness of a pipeline is often measured by the number of instructions a processor can compute per clock cycle. A "superscalar" processor can execute more than one instruction per clock cycle which is achieved with pipelining. Modern microprocessor pipelines can include dozens of pipeline stages, but even the most complex pipelines categorize the stages into instruction fetching, decoding and initializing control logic, data access, execution, and writing the results back to memory.

Unfortunately, controlling the pipelining of machine instructions is extremely complex compared to the pipeline associated with manufacturing assembly lines. It is often the case that the pipeline must "stall" because instructions often have special exceptions or need to use a stage of a pipeline for a prolonged period of time (prolonged in comparison to a Ghz at least). Some modern processors dedicate tremendous control logic which takes up precious chip real-estate and power consumption for the sole purpose of controlling pipelines. The popularity of dual pipelines in modern processors certainly contributes to this.

(16)
Type: Knowledge-based

Hint: Digital is to discrete and finite as analog is to continuous and periodic.

Hint: The majority of circuitry today is digital.

Solution: Analog circuits use variable signaling to produce a continuous variable output. An analog signal is composed of AC and DC magnitudes, phase, and frequency. The first computers used analog circuitry. Analog circuits are often composed with components such as diodes, potentiometers, operational amplifiers, resistors, and capacitors. Analog computation is greatly hindered by undesirable effects such as noise.

Digital circuits are a subset of traditional circuits which only produce two outputs voltage levels. These voltage levels are often considered High/Low or 1/0. This simplifies theory for circuit design because the logic levels are binary. Many of the operations performed in digital circuits assume primitives called logic gates. Examples of logic gates are OR gates (outputs 1 if any input is 1), AND gates (outputs 1 only if all inputs are also 1), and Inverters (outputs the opposite of the input). Examples of circuitry that uses digital logic are microprocessors and random access memory (RAM).

(17)
Type: Design problem

Hint: It is critical that you don't assume the input sizes of the OR gates and decoder without asking the interviewer. They can be of the size you see fit.

Hint: A truth table is a good way to start. A kaurnaugh map (K-Map) is not necessary.

Solution: A 1-bit full adder has two inputs for binary addition as well as a carry input and output. See Figure 9-3.

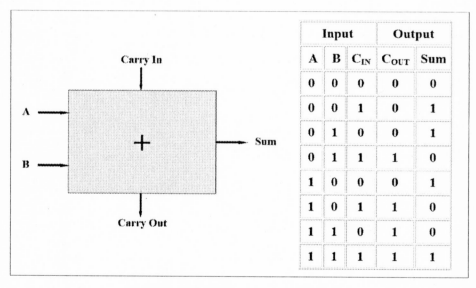

Input			Output	
A	B	C_{IN}	C_{OUT}	Sum
0	0	0	0	0
0	0	1	0	1
0	1	0	0	1
0	1	1	1	0
1	0	0	0	1
1	0	1	1	0
1	1	0	1	0
1	1	1	1	1

Figure 9-3. Full adder diagram and truth table

Regardless of how you order the inputs and outputs of the truth table, it should become clear that C_{out} and Sum both have four rows that result in a true (or high voltage) output. The boolean equations according to the true outputs follow:

$$\text{Sum} = \overline{A}BC_{in} + A\overline{B}C_{in} + AB\overline{C}_{in} + \overline{ABC}_{in}$$

$$C_{out} = \overline{A}BC_{in} + A\overline{B}C_{in} + AB\overline{C}_{in} + \overline{AB}C_{in}$$

A decoder with A, B, and C_{in} has an output corresponding to each of the ANDed expressions above. Thus, a 4-bit OR gate can be used for both Sum and C_{out} as shown in Figure 9-4 to build a 1-bit full adder. If you want to be fancy, you can use a 3-bit OR gate by simplifying the equation for C_{out}.

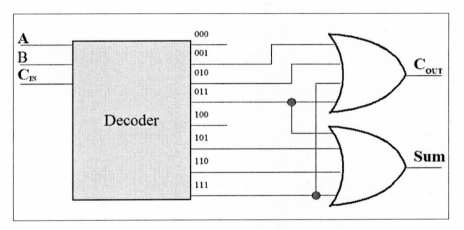

Figure 9-4. Solution using a 3-bit decoder and 4-bit OR gates

(18)
Type: Knowledge-based

Hint: The interviewer is referring to different strategies for storing information in cache memory.

Hint: A simple scheme is to use direct mapping.

Solution: Consider the following approaches:

- *Direct-mapping.* This is a simple approach to caching which maps each address in the cache to an equal portion of higher-level memory. For example, if you have a cache of four entries and system memory of forty entries (for the sake of discussion), the first address of the cache would be mapped to memory addresses 0-9 of the system memory, the second to 10-19, and so forth. The advantage to this approach is that detecting a cache "hit" or "miss" is very fast as only a small portion of the cache is searched. The disadvantage is not all the cache may be utilized since each memory location in higher-level memory (such as system memory) has only one memory location in the cache to utilize. This approach performs better as the size of cache memory increases proportionate to the higher-level memory it services.

- *Fully-associative.* In a fully associative cache there are no rules as to where a recently fetched higher-level memory entry can go in the cache. This approach ensures that the entire cache's memory is always utilized, but usually results in scanning the entire cache before detecting a cache miss. Generally this scheme is most effective for very small caches.

- *Set-associative.* This is a compromise between the two previous approaches. A set is defined which is usually a power of 2 such as 4, 8, etc. Each memory address of the higher-level memory is assigned to a set. Thus, instead of having only one memory location to use in the cache as in the direct-mapping scheme, each memory address from the higher-level memory can be placed anywhere within a set of locations in the cache (usually overwriting the oldest entry).

Note: The following programming solutions follow the top-down, comments-to-pseudo code approach discussed in the "Programming questions" section.

(19)
Type: Programming

Hint: If you are stuck, draw a linked list and do it by hand first.

Hint: Consider an iterative solution.

Solution: An iterative solution involves changing the direction of the "links" between elements using very little memory compared to recursion. This solution assumes the linked list's head element is known and the tail element links to null:

```
/* create and initialize references that will traverse linked list */
Element runner = head. next
Element follower = head

/* create bookkeeping temporary variable */
Element temp

/* first element is a special case */
head Node. next = null

/* iterate through linked list until the end is reached */
while (runner != null) {

        //save the reference for the element after the runner
        temp = runner. next

        //reverse the runner's link
        runner. next = follower

        //increment the position for runner and follower
        follower = runner
        runner = temp

}
```

Follow-up question: Is an iterative solution best under all circumstances?

Follow-up solution: As is the case for most programming problems, the best solution is dependent on the requirements, computer architecture, programming language, etc. There are circumstances where a recursive solution solves the problem just as well. Many functional languages (and many mixed-paradigm languages like C/C++) can automatically convert tail recursion into iteration. In this case, a solution using the following recursive function performs similarly, but is more readable and maintainable:

```
/* recursive function that reverses the link between two nodes */
void reverse (Element element, Element follower)
{

    //save element linked to follower
    temp = follower. next

    //reverse link between the given element and the follower
    follower. next = element

    //recur when the given element has a following element
    if (element. next != null) {
        reverse (element. next, temp)

    }

}
```

(20)
Type: Programming

Hint: Think of the characters in the magazine as a set or collection.

Hint: The set of usable characters can include repeating characters. For example, if there is only one 'z' in the magazine, a message with "zeuz" is not possible.

Solution: Clearly, searching the set of characters in the magazine for each character in the ransom note is inefficient. The following solution uses a lookup table to hold the number of each character in the magazine. Once the lookup table is populated, the set of characters in the ransom note are traversed and the corresponding entry in the lookup table is decremented. If the algorithm attempts to decrement an entry in the lookup table below zero, assembly of the ransom note is not possible.

Method to determine if ransom note can be assembled

```
Boolean canBeAssembled (Set magazine, Set ransom Note) {

    /* create lookup table */
    LTable lTable = new LTable ()

    /* populate lookup table */
    for (char current Char : magazine) {
        lTable. add (current Char)

    }

    /* iterate through ransom Note */
    for (char current Char : ransom Note) {

    //decrement count for current Char, if unavailable return false
    if (!LTable. decrement (current Char))
        return false

    }

    /* return true since every ransom note character available */
    return true

}
```

Lookup table implementation

```
LTable {

    /* create container to represent table data */
    int DynamicArray lookupData = new DynamicArray ()

    /* method to increment count for character */
    add (char c) {

        //cast to integer to get ascii or unicode index
        int index = (int) c

        //get the element at the index
        int element = lookupData.get (index)
```

```
            //if the position in the array is null insert an integer of 1:
            if (element == null)
                lookupData.add (index, 1)

            //otherwise increment the existing integer
            else
                lookupData.add (index, ++element)

            }

            /* method to check and decrement character availability */
            boolean decrement (char c) {

            //cast to integer representation
            int index = (int) c

            //get corresponding character count
            int element = lookupData.get (index)

            //if available decrement and return true
            if (element != null and element > 0) {
                element--
                return true

            }

            //otherwise return false
            else
                return false

        }

    }
```

This solution provides some very good talking points to show your industry perspective. In the real world, a library class could be used such as Map or Hash Map to replace the implementation of the lookup table. Of course, this would push some of the implementation of the custom lookup table such as decrementing a character's count to the can BeAssembled method.

The pseudo code for the lookup table implementation assumes a dynamic array is available (an array that resizes itself as needed). If the size of the character set is known (such as standard ascii which is 127 characters), an array of the given size may prove to be most efficient as the array indexes would correspond to character codes (a chain or linked list is inefficient because random access is needed).

(21)
Type: Programming

Hint: Recursion is not recommended.

Hint: Although there is no linear or quadratic solution, organizing the puzzle pieces ahead of time can greatly influence the speed of the searches for interlocking pieces.

Solution: There is no way to eliminate searching several piece sides to find matches, but you can divide all the puzzle sides into different sets so not all of them have to be searched each time. Additionally, you can ensure puzzle sides that have already been matched are not redundantly searched again. The following solution organizes the puzzle piece sides into three lists of sides—edge Sides, inner Sides, and outer Sides.

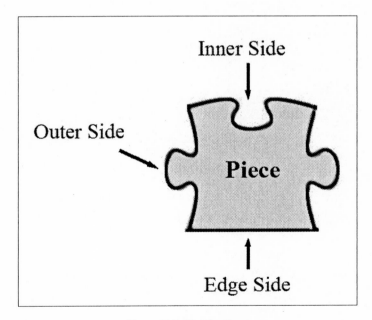

Figure 9-5. Puzzle piece

The algorithm starts with the bottom-left corner and proceeds to assemble the entire edge of the puzzle. As every new pieces is added to the puzzle, its sides are removed from the sets. Thus, the searches get faster as the puzzle is assembled. When the outer perimeter is finished, the inner pieces are assembled starting from the bottom-right corner again from left to right by row as shown in Figure 9-6.

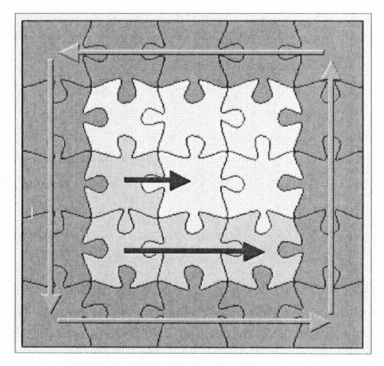

Figure 9-6. Puzzle assembly algorithm in progress

The light arrows in Figure 9-6 illustrate the assembly of the perimeter and the dark arrows depict the inner piece assembly by row.

Some drawings on a white board and a bit of code to explain how you would develop the main algorithm at a high-level is probably all an interviewer would be interested in (no one should be expected to write all the of the following code in less than an hour), but a more complete solution follows:

The primary algorithm

```
/* create and populate lists, assumes side classes are given */
List edgeSides = populateEdgeSides (allSides)
List innerSides = populateInnerSides (allSides)
List outerSides = populateOuterSides (allSides)

/* assemble perimeter and create reference to first non-edge piece */
Piece current = assemblePerimeter (bottomLeftCorner, edgeSides,
innerSides, outerSides)

/* initialize bookkeeping variables to save the first piece in a row and
results from searches for interlocking pieces */
Piece firstInRow = current
Piece match

/* iterate until side lists are empty */
while (innerSides.NotEmpty or outerSides.NotEmpty) {

    //if current piece has an inner side, search for match in outer list
    //find method reduces future searches by removing side from list
    if (current.right == InnerSide)
        match = findAndRemoveMatch (current.right, outerSides)

    //otherwise search in inner list
    else
        match = findAndRemoveMatch (current.right, innerSides)

    //if an interlocking piece is found, add the new piece to the puzzle
    if (match != null) {
        puzzle.interlock (current.right, match)
        current = match
    }
```

```
        //if no match is found, the row is complete
        //find the next row's first piece
        else {

            if (firstInRow.top == InnerSide)
                match = findAndRemoveMatch (firstInRow.top, outerSides)
            else
                match = findAndRemoveMatch (firstInRow.top, innerSides)

            //add match to puzzle
            puzzle.interlock

            //update first In Row and current
            firstInRow, current = match.piece
        }

    }
```

Worker method to populate list of edge sides

```
/* This method returns a the list of all edge sides. The populateOuter-
Sides and populateInnerSides methods are omitted as they are identical
after isEdgeSide is replaced. */

List populateSides (List allSides) {

    /* create output list */
    List matchingSides

    /* iterate through all available sides */
    for (Side current : allSides) {

        //insert matching sides into output list
        if (current == EdgeSide)
            matchingSides.add(current)

    }

    return matchingSides

}
```

Worker method that assembles the perimeter

```
/* This method assembles the outer edge pieces and returns the bottom-
left non-edge piece */

Piece assemblePerimeter (Piece bottomLeftCorner, List edgeSides, List
innerSides, List outerSides) {

    /* create bookkeeping variables */
    Piece current, match

    /* assemble to the right until the bottom-right corner is reached */
    do while (current != Corner) {

        //find a piece that interlocks with current piece from edge list
        //reduce future searches by removing right side from edge list
        match = findAndRemoveMatch (current.right, edgeSides)
        puzzle.interlock (current.right, match)
    }
    /* assemble upward until top-right corner is reached */
    do while (current != Corner) {
    match = findAndRemoveMatch (current.top, edgeSides)
    puzzle.interlock (current.top, match)
    }
    /* assemble to the left until top-left corner is reached */
    do while (current != Corner) {
        match = findAndRemoveMatch (current.left, edgeSides)
        puzzle.interlock (current.left, match)
    }
    /* assemble downward until bottom-left corner is reached again */
    do while (current != Corner) {
        match = findAndRemoveMatch (current.bottom, edgeSides)
        puzzle.interlock (current.bottom, match)
    }
    /* perimeter is assembled, now assemble the bottom-left non-edge
    piece and return it */
    if(current.right == InnerSide)
        match = findAndRemoveMatch (current.right, outerSides)
```

```
    if (current.right == OuterSide)
        match = findAndRemoveMatch (current.right, innerSides)

    /* add first non-perimeter piece to puzzle and return it */
    puzzle.interlock (current.right, match)
    return match.parentPiece

}
```

Worker method to find a matching side and remove it from its respective list

```
Side findAndRemoveMatch(Side givenSide, List searchList) {

    /* iterate over given list */
    for (Side current : searchList) {

        //use function given by interviewer to determine a match
        if (piecesInterlock(current, givenSide)) {

            //remove from the search list and return it
            searchList.remove(current)
            return current

        }

    }

}
```

There certainly are plenty of insights to be made about this problem for a healthy discussion with the interviewer. If performance is of paramount concern and seperate computing agents are available, the puzzle could be assembled in parallel starting at each corner. Also, even though recursion may seem like the most natural solution with a breath-first search (BFS) or depth-first search (DFS), it is not possible without a great deal of memory because of cycles.

The puzzle is really a graph where any four nodes are part of a cycle. Routing algorithms could be used, but it would be costly in the memory domain compared to an iterative solution. Something else to note is that the above algorithm would fail on the fourth line on special cases such as a jig-saw puzzle with only one or two pieces.

(22)
Type: Programming

Hint: The solution is not recursive.

Hint: Try using a queue.

Solution: Similar to how you need a queue to do a breath-first search on a graph, traversing a tree by levels requires a queue. The following solution continuously removes the current visible element from the queue, inserts the element's children into the queue, and prints the element. A variable keeps track of the first element for each level so the algorithms knows when to print a new line. Additionally, a queue from a standard library is assumed to be available. See Figure 9-7.

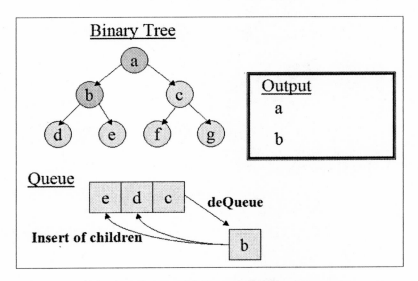

Figure 9-7. Solution to binary tree algorithm in progress

```
/* create first node of next level bookkeeping variable */
Node firstInNextLevel

/* print the root */
print root

/* insert children of the root, if they exist, into the queue */
if (root.Left Child != null) {
    queue.offer(root.LeftChild)
    queue.offer(root.RightChild)
}

/* initialize first of next level */
firstInNextLevel = root.LeftChild

/* create variable that will traverse queue */
Node currentElement

/* iterate until all the nodes are printed or the queue is empty */
while(queue.NotEmpty) {

    //remove visible element from queue
    currentElement = queue.remove()

    //special case when first node of next level is encountered
    if (currentElement == firstInNextLevel) {

        //start a new line
        print new line

        //update level reference to left child of current element
        firstInNextLevel = firstInNextLine.leftChild

    }

    /* print removed element */
    print currentElement

    /* insert children into the queue, if they exist */
    if (currentElement.leftChild != null) {
        queue.offer(currentElemen.leftChild)
        queue.offer(currentElement.right Child)
    }

}
```

(23)
Type: Knowledge-based

Hint: Transistors are often used in amplifiers for analog circuitry.

Hint: The invention of transistors gave rise to the advent of digital logic.

Solution: A transistor is a semiconductor device that has three terminals. One terminal can control the flow of current or voltage (dependent on the type) across the remaining two terminals. There are various types of transistors including field-effect transistors (FET) and bipolar junction transistors (BJT).

BJTs control the amplification of current across its "emitter" and "collector" terminals. A simplified way to describe a bipolar junction transistor is to consider it a variable resistor controlled by current.

Field-effect transistors are the most common category of transistor used today and are often found in integrated circuits. Given an input current, this family of transistors creates an electric field which in-effect generates a second electric current across the transistor. The new electric current is often amplified compared to the input current. The signal is commonly connected to the "gate" terminal and an output signal is used either from the "source" or "drain" terminals. FETs are commonly used as switches in digital circuits facilitating binary logic and as amplifiers in analog circuits.

The most common type of modern FET transistors are Metal Oxide Semiconductor FET (MOSFET). The reason they are so popular is that they are the building blocks for CMOS circuits which limit the flow of current facilitating virtually no power consumption unless a logic gate is switched.

(24)
Type: Design problem

Hint: Think about how you would reduce power consumption or dissipation for any circuit.

Hint: Microcontrollers are made from CMOS circuitry.

Solution: A necessarily brief description of various techniques follows. Don't be discouraged by these textbook definitions. The real objective of this question is to have a healthy discussion; if you are able to hint at even a few of the following points you are in good shape.

- *Use an asynchronous circuit design.* A synchronous circuit uses a clock which forces CMOS circuitry to switch on every clock cycle. An asynchronous design drives logic only when work needs to be done capitalizing on the low static power consumption of CMOS circuitry.

- *Clock gating.* Power can be saved by disabling logic that is not currently being used. This technique disables a clock when a circuit component is not used. A simple way to do this is to use an AND gate with an enable signal and the clock as inputs.

- *Reducing leakage.* When current passes that is not intended to do so (usually by parasitic capacitance and sub threshold conduction), this is called leakage. A common technique for reducing leakage is to use longer channel length transistors.

- *Reduce operating frequency.* If the circuit doesn't need a high clock frequency then reduce it. For example, the clock for a counter may only require 4Mhz instead of 33Mhz. The clock can also be turned off when not used.

- *Reduce the supply voltage.* This creates a trade-off, because as voltage decreases, the delay of the circuit increases. Thus, the designer can add redundant or parallel circuitry to compensate and reduce power consumption.

- *Reduce capacitance.* Capacitors store energy, thus more capacitance means more power consumption. Try to reduce capacitance wherever possible, especially in high frequency sections. For example, for an RC oscillator, using a small capacitor and a large resistor could save power consumption.

- *Input signal transition speed.* If an input to a CMOS circuit takes a long time to change state (rise or fall), the transistors spend more time carrying current which consumes more energy. Generally, the faster the transition time the better. Floating inputs (unconnected) can also create unnecessary power consumption.

(25)
Type: Knowledge-based

Hint: The interviewer is referring to filtering signal frequencies.

Hint: An example is a low-pass filter.

Solution: Consider the following list of filters for signal processing:

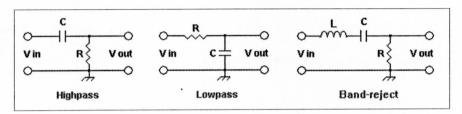

Figure 9-8. Circuit diagrams for first-order filters

- *Band-pass.* This filter only allows frequencies within two bounds or a "band" to propagate through the circuit.

- *Band-reject.* All frequencies are allowed except those within a given band.

- *High-pass.* Only frequencies greater than a certain bound are allowed.

- *Low-pass.* Frequencies below a given bound can pass through the circuit.

A talking point for this would be that all of the filter circuit diagrams are first order meaning they gradually filter out undesired frequencies over time. Most modern filters almost immediately react to changes in frequencies in a discrete rather than analog fashion. Additionally, the described filters use only resistors, inductors, and capacitors. There are various ways to make filters including the use of op-amps, complex analog or digital control, etc.

Finally, don't fret too much about the circuit diagrams. Just knowing that RC (and LRC) circuits can create filters is probably all you would need to know initially. In a real interview, the interviewer is your guide.

(26)
Type: Knowledge-based

Hint: This question has to do with the study of solid-state semiconductors.

Hint: The interviewer is referring to the polarity of transistors.

Solution: N-type and P-type refer to the two types of bipolar transistors. N-type or N channel transistors refer to a layering of neutral, positive, and neutral semiconductor material. The P-doped or boron doped layer is often called the base and is sandwiched between two N-doped or arsenic doped layers.

NPN transistors are the most common used today considering that they are more easily constructed with silicon. A P-type or PNP transistor is the opposite where the middle layer is N-doped. The only functional difference between them is the direction of the current flow in the emitter terminal. Thus, a PNP transistor can be used in the same fashion as an NPN transistor if the wiring to two of the terminals is switched.

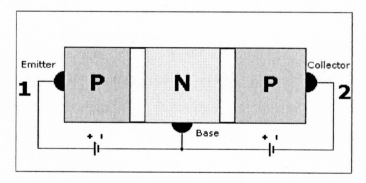

Figure 9-9. P-type or PNP bi-polar transistor

(27)
Type: Knowledge-based

Hint: These are the fundamentals of the theory of constraints (TOC).

Hint: Inventory and expenses have a very intuitive meaning.

Solution: Consider these talking points rather than definitions:

- *Throughput.* Rate at which the manufacturing firm sells finished goods (this is not synonymous with a manufacturing production rate).

- *Inventory.* The money the firm has invested in purchasing things which it intends to sell. These include raw materials, components, and finished goods that have been bought by the firm, but not yet sold (this does not include labor and overhead costs).

- *Operating Expenses.* Cost of converting inventory into throughput. This includes direct and indirect labor costs.

(28)
Type: Technical case

Hint: It is often the goal to maximize the productivity of an assembly line.

Hint: Before assigning tasks to workers in an assembly line, some facts need to be collected.

Solution: Assembly operation is the process of combining the parts of a product in a systematic and orderly fashion. One of the important tasks in manufacturing environment is to design assembly lines in such a way that the demands for the products are met and the productivity of the assembly line is maximized. The following is a summary of a possible assembly line balancing procedure:

- Establish the list of tasks involved in the assembly process.

- Estimate required time for each task.

- Determine the precedence relationships between the tasks.

- Determine the cycle time required to meet the desired production rate.

- Assign the tasks to stations by using a assembly line balancing heuristic.

(29)
Type: Knowledge-based

Hint: How does energy flow through metals?

Hint: One method is radiation.

Solution: The three modes of head transfer are convection, conduction, and radiation:

- *Convection.* When fluid is in motion and adjacent to a solid, energy is transferred.

- *Conduction.* Conduction is the flow of energy through solids. It is either associated with free flowing electrons within a solid (common in metals) or the transfer of energy from fast moving molecules to less-energetic molecules.

- *Radiation.* Energy is transferred outside of a medium over a wavelength. Shorter wavelengths such as those associated with Gamma-rays can carry more energy.

(29)
Type: Knowledge-based

Hint: Tremendous pressure is commonly associated with static failure.

Hint: "Wear and tear" should come to mind when considering fatigue failure.

Solution: When some combination of principle forces on a material become too great, a static failure occurs such as buckling or shearing. Fatigue failure is associated with repeated cycling of load. The metal incurs progressive damage due to fluctuations in stress.

COMMON MISTAKES

1. *Making poor assumptions.* Even in knowledge-based questions, making poor assumptions can squander a lot of your time. A good practice is to state your assumptions back to the interviewer.

2. *Trying to immediately give an answer.* Concentrate on a plan to show the interviewer that you are a strong problem solver rather than trying to produce an answer immediately. Even if you are certain of the solution from the start, take some time to explain the series of logical steps you used or, if appropriate, expand on the solution showing the interviewer your industry perspective.

3. *Objecting that the question has nothing to do with the job.* It's okay to be honest and state something like "Interesting. That's the most bazaar question I've had yet," but avoid using your opinion as a basis for not attempting to answer the question. While the details may indeed have nothing to do with the job, your motivation and ability to solve new problems does.

4. *Trying to answer a question without first fully understanding what is being asked.* If you don't understand a word in the question or aren't entirely sure what is being asked, begin by gaining a clear understanding of the requirements before approaching a solution.

5. *Preparing too much and focusing on the wrong material.* There are various forms of preparation that can make a significant difference for a technical interview such as company research, answering sample questions orally, and developing your custom approach to technical questions. However, there is little value in memorizing question banks or reviewing years of coursework. Interviews are not exams—they are discussions.

Profile
Benjamin Lewis

Who do you work for, what is your official job title, and where is the job located?

I'm a Software Design Engineer for Microsoft in Redmond, Washington. I'm part of the Xbox™ Live Team.

Was it your first choice?

Yes. It was the first job I applied for which I gladly took. I didn't even bother looking for anything else.

What are some positive aspects of the job?

I think Microsoft treats its employees right and has a strong focus on making sure we are happy. My manager constantly is asking how we are doing. I get free drinks at the office and the benefits package is top of the line.

There are sports teams to get involved with—I personally play Magic every week with a group of guys. So, it's easy to find a community. I come into work whenever I wanted to, take off my shoes, hang around, and wear whatever is comfortable. Also, we are the first to beta test various Xbox games. When I'm given an assignment sometimes I'm given a deadline, but it is usually left to my discretion and judgment. Most of all, I get to work with very smart, entertaining people.

What are some negative aspects?

It is definitely your stereotypical programming job—I'm a code monkey. I'm given a spec and write some code to meet that spec. There is very little creativity involved. Microsoft is such a giant company that I feel that I'm making a minimal impact. Work is spread around so many people that you feel you are not accomplishing much.

What is your typical day like?

I get up, watch the practice, and get to work around 11:00 to 11:30. I grab a coffee with hot chocolate, check email, look at last night's check in list, and bug list. After a bit, I formulate a plan for my day.

Lunch is usually around 1:00 to 1:30. After lunch I start working on my bug list or spec list. 95% of the code I write is in C#. I have meetings just about everyday. For example, I may have a program manager meeting where we talk about an upcoming project or a meeting with the development team.

Sometimes I play foosball or Mario Tennis with the OPS Team who are the guys that actually run the Xbox Live servers. The OPS team uses the software that I write. I usually leave around 6 PM. Sometimes I come in on weekends if there is a lot of work to do. My time during a typical day usually breaks down as follows:

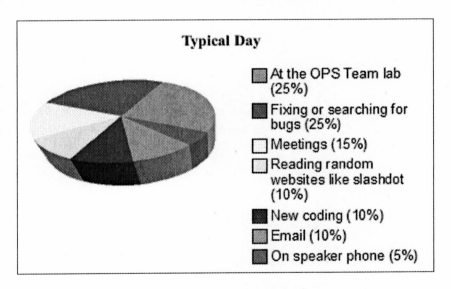

How did you make initial contact with Microsoft?

I submitted a four page resume to them during my freshman year at a career fair. They offered me a campus interview where I wrote a string function. I then flew out for site interviews with Office for the Mac and another group which I can't remember right now.

I turned them down because I wanted to concentrate on starting a dot-com company at the time. During my junior year, however, I flew over again and Interviewed for the Xbox Live team and the games team. I decided to take the internship this time for which I received a 5/5 rating and later accepted my current position after graduating.

How did you prepare for your interviews?

I didn't prepare much except for looking at grey labyrinth to get familiar with puzzle questions in my spare time. I walked in to each of my interviews dressed in my usual casual college attire, put my stuffed monkey on the table, and asked what questions they had for us.

What were you interviews like?

I had five interviews—one HR and the rest technical. I would say the tech interviews were 60% technical and 40% behavioral. They were in an office setting by full-time employees. Each interview became deeper and deeper technically to test my quality as a coder.

Have any memorable questions?

Imagine that you have a linked list that is either without cycles or shaped like a 'P.' How do you determine which? After trying a lot of memory inefficient methods and receiving a few hints, I figured out that you can use two pointers where one is incremented twice as fast as the other.

What is the fastest way to reverse a byte? The first thing I said was "Well, in the real world the fastest way would be to use a lookup table or array with 256 entries." The interviewer smiled and stopped me by saying "That's what I was looking for—let's move on."

Did you ever encounter a question you didn't know how to solve?

Usually the questions are easy to solve with a slow or memory intensive solution—start with that. They will guide you and give you hints when you're not making progress. Talk to them like they are human beings. For example, "Well, I know you want me to do this in linear time, but the best thing that comes to mind is this..." Always have a conversation. They are looking for an engaging discussion coder-to-coder, not answers to a multiple choice test.

Have any other advice on approaching technical questions?

Think out loud, appear confident but not arrogant, and have a positive attitude. Talk about side projects or things you've done in the past that is relevant to the question—anything that shows you tinker in your field for fun.

Note: At the time of this book's publication, Benjamin Lewis went on to business school at the University of Michigan.

BENJAMIN LEWIS

1010 Catherine, 205 • Ann Arbor, MI 48104
bdl@umich.edu • 734.657.4910

EDUCATION	**UNIVERSITY OF MICHIGAN**	**Ann Arbor, MI**

University of Michigan Business School
Master of Business Administration, May 2005
- Emphasis in Technology Commercialization
- Winner of the ZLI Entrepreneurial Scholarship and UMBS Merit Scholarship (awarded to top 15 students based on academics and leadership)
- Won the Dare to Dream Business Plan Competition resulting in a $10,000 grant
- Semifinalist in Thunderbird Innovation Challenge Competition
- Took Second Place at UMBS in the Walter V. Shipley Ethical Case Competition
- First place at UMBS in E-Strat Loreal Marketing Competition

College of Engineering
Bachelor of Science in Computer Engineering, December 2001
- Distinguished Achievement Award (ranked 1st in the major)
- Summa Cum Laude (3.9/4.0)

EXPERIENCE **Summer 2004**	**IBM**	**Austin, TX**

Extreme Blue Product Manager Intern, Team Outspoken
- Created a business plan for IBM multimodal techology, a new way of accessing the internet on mobile devices with a speech-in, speech-out interface in addition to the traditional keypad-in, screen-out interface, which outlined the technology commercialization strategy.
- Led a team of five engineers to create a proof-of-concept multimodal application which won runner-up for best demo at Sizzling Tech Expo and is used in sales pitches to drive demand in external partners and consumers.
- Produced a product demonstration video and corresponding sales pitch that led to multiple partnerships in adopting IBM multimodal technology.
- Created seven multimodal patent invention disclosures which will give IBM a competitive advantage in selling this technology.

2002-2003	**MICROSOFT CORPORATION**	**Redmond, WA**

Software Design Engineer
- Designed and developed tools that stabilized the 500,000+ member Xbox Live service.
- Collaborated with the operations team to streamline maintenance and created the largest tool for the online team that reduced downtime and upgrade time by over 90%.

2000-2002	**BIDCENTIVES.COM**	**Ann Arbor, MI**

Founder and Chief Technical Officer
- Developed efficient textbook trading strategy and highly effective web marketing strategy, adding new users for less than fifty-cents per user in marketing spend.
- Raised $235,000 in angel funding to start BidCentives.com, which provided cost-effective marketing to fledgling internet sites.
- Led team of twelve programmers and designers to create an application framework that generated multi-digit growth per month in active users for our clients.
- Worked with client sites in order to generate exponential growth through custom programming and services.
- Sold company for a profit

1999-2001	**PC-HUG DEVELOPMENT GROUP**	**Ann Arbor, MI**

Founder, Chief Executive Officer
- Coordinated work between clients and web designers, worked on design specifications, customer relations, and sales.
- Clients including Macomb Community College, Henry Ford Hospital, law firms, and medical practices.

ADDITIONAL	• Teacher's assistant for a programming course for non-engineers at the University of Michigan.

10

Understanding Human Resources—HR Interviews, Salary Negotiation, & More

Students are often under the impression that a human resource representative is just an administrative assistant who handles logistics and occasionally collects resumes. You may be surprised to find out the strategic nature of modern human resource organizations. HR has become an executive management discipline of paramount concern to businesses. According to "Microsoft: Competing on Talent," a case study by Harvard Business School Publishing, a company's HR organization is often at the core of its competitive advantage.

Your strategy for presenting yourself and communicating with HR representatives should be significantly different than your interactions with hiring managers. In many cases, the HR organization is completely separate from the professional workforce and has very different motives when considering new-hire candidates. This chapter cuts through the self-promotion and marketing that employers use to describe their HR divisions and explains their underlying purpose, what they are looking for when you interact with them, and how to deal with issues such as competing offers and compensation.

WHY ORGANIZATIONS HAVE HUMAN RESOURCE DIVISIONS

From the standpoint of business management, employees are often seen as investments to create profit for stakeholders. Just like investing in a stock or a home, business management seeks to gain the most potential value at the lowest price. This is often the internal mission statement of a human resources organization. Many executive HR officers refer to hiring and training employees as growing "human capital."

HR organizations often consider hiring managers their customers. The HR organization specializes in attracting suitable candidates and accommodating managers by professionally producing pools of potential candidates on-demand.

It can be helpful to have some background information on what motivates HR organizations. Consider the following metrics by which a professional HR organization is measured:

- *Retention and Attrition.* Retention is the percentage of employees that stay in the organization over a given period of time. Attrition is the running percentage of employees that leave the company and are replaced. When retention is low and turnover is high, it reflects very poorly on an HR organization. It is very expensive to hire and train an employee. Partially depending on the effectiveness of an HR organization, the average cost of hiring someone is 50% to 150% percent of their yearly salary including the cost of the interview process, training, the new hire's initial un-productivity, etc. Not all attrition is bad, in fact sometimes it is planned to ensure only the highest performers are employed.

  According to the department of labor (http://www.bls.gov/jlt/home.htm), there is over a 20% turnover rate on-average for professional employees in the United States. For many companies, the most expensive cost for doing business is their workforce. When turnover rates change they generate waves for their most expensive cost and an HR organization is often held accountable.

- *Attraction.* This is the number of potential candidates the HR organization attracts for recruiting. If the business needs to hire in order to keep up with customer demand, it is often the HR organization's responsibility to attract eligible candidates. If the organization loses business because of staffing problems, it often reflects poorly on HR.

- *Hire-on percentage.* The hire-on percentage is a rating of how many candidates accept a position. A low hire-on percentage means more candidates need to go through the expensive interview process or positions remain open reducing productivity.

- *Compliance.* There are many regulations that HR organizations need to follow by law, most notably, Equal Opportunity compliance. HR organizations are very aware of such regulations and try to mitigate the risk of being sued.

- *Wage inflation.* It is often the goal of an HR organization to have a candidate accept an offer at the lowest possible price. The organization may be motivated to showcase non-monetary compensation such as flexible work hours and downplay salary or bonuses. In some companies, the pay scales have been stagnant for years meaning a competitive new-hire compensation package according to today's standards falls into their more experienced pay grades. When a college candidate is hired, the organization may have to bump the new hire to a higher pay grade in order to be competitive which may disqualify them from promotions for years. This is what is meant by wage inflation. Although they are important to be aware of, these practices should not concern a college hire as much as more experienced hires, because most organizations have standardized compensation rates for university hiring.

Most HR representatives claim they are there to help you and be your advocate during the hiring process. After reading the above metrics, it should be clear that in most cases it is in the best interest for an HR representative to help you, but not always. For example, in an effort to increase the attraction rate, or the pool of available candidates to managers, a recruiter may lead you on just to increase their database count. It is important to understand that a recruiting/staffing person's performance depends on the metrics.

The next section explains how you can use this more realistic perspective of a human resource organization to your advantage.

HUMAN RESOURCE INTERVIEWS

Human resource interviews are often by phone or are 30-minute office interviews. Of course, they are not called HR interviews by employers, but after reading this section you will be aware when you are asked an HR-related question. It is common to get HR questions from hiring mangers as well mixed in with behavioral or technical questions.

To best illustrate how to handle common HR interview questions, consider the following list:

Why do you want to work for us?

Translation: If we offer you a job will you take it?

Strategy: Show them that you want the job and that you are serious. Anything that shows you have respect for the organization or that you admire it should be stated. Consider the following sample answer:

> *When I think of Red hat, I see a company that is forging the path for the information age. Its products are world renowned and I believe in them because I've been using one version of Red hat or another for years. Working for you would be a chance to be in the same organization as some of the finest developers in the world.*

Do you have competing offers?

Translation: Are you out of our league?

Strategy: This is one of the most difficult HR questions to answer. You need to weigh showing that you are in high demand against showing that you are truly interested in working for them. If it is a large company that often hires top candidates, it is usually safe to tell them who their competition is. However, if it is a smaller company, especially during a screening interview, they may have a policy where they do not bring candidates in for site interviews if they have competing offers. Here is a sample answer:

> *I am considering other opportunities at Raytheon and a smaller company called Citrix, but to be honest, I am far more excited about your organization.*

Here is a sample answer in the case that the candidate does not have competing offers:

> *I'm considering various job leads, but my job search is still in the early stages. I'll have to see how those leads mature. I have to admit, this position is the most exciting opportunity I could expect.*

What are the other companies offering?

Translation: Are you in our target range?

Strategy: Defer all salary negotiation until you have an offer in writing. The following section, "Negotiating Compensation," will discuss this in more detail.

Do you want to go back to school full-time?

Translation: Are we going to lose our investment in you before it yields profit?

Strategy: Although you may want to show that you have great aspirations to get a doctorate degree, this is the worst thing to say unless it's completely true that you intend to pursue an additional degree as a full-time student. Emphasize that you are looking for a good organization to build a career with and add value to. For example:

> *Perhaps I'll go back to school someday, but for the foreseeable future, I want to establish a good career and learn as much as I can in industry.*

What is your five year plan?

Translation: Are you going to use us for a few years and then leave?

Strategy: Organizations are often looking for a productive worker that they can retain. One approach is to show that you have aspirations to be a great leader within their organization, but are willing to work hard and start at the bottom:

> *Well, I hope to join an organization full of opportunity such as yours and spend my early years learning as much as I can while adding value to that organization. Then hopefully by rising to a leadership role after some solid experience, I can be*

even more influential in helping the organization, it's customers, and my fellow workers achieve success.

NEGOTIATING COMPENSATION

Before you consider negotiation of compensation, be sure you think about the trade-offs associated with it—with compensation comes more responsibility. Do you want your manager's expectations to be higher for you than that for other new-hires? For example, would you be willing to work longer hours than your peers?

Some candidates are ready to take on extra responsibility, but fear that it is rude or arrogant to attempt to negotiate. The truth is, the majority of candidates do some form of negotiation, even if it's just pointing out a comparison to the average base salary of their field. You've worked very hard for your degree and have every right to make sure you are offered the job you deserve.

If you decide you want to negotiate, there is one rule that is so crucial for monetary negotiation that it requires special emphasis:

The key to salary negotiation

Avoid salary negotiation until you have read every word of the offer letter.

Do not discuss salary until you have an offer in writing. In some cases, you may want to wait until you have additional leverage such as a competing offer. Until you have an offer letter, you have nothing to negotiate with the employer—the ball is in their court. As tempted as you may be to bring it up, there is absolutely nothing you can gain by discussing it prematurely.

HR representatives often attempt to find out your salary expectations during screening interviews. If you give them a number, it can only serve to your disadvantage because it is often the goal of an HR representative to hire you at the lowest possible price. Thus, if a number is disclosed, the candidate has little hope of negotiating anything higher or in the worst case—the HR representative may discontinue the interview process if your off-hand expectations are higher than their targets.

Some human resource organizations even tailor offers to exploit premature candidate expectations. For example, an HR organization may react to an expectation of a 60,000 dollar base salary by meeting it, but also by excluding eligibility for a signing bonus, relocation bonus, stock options, etc. Since many college hires only consider base salary, they can end up accepting offers that are grossly reduced in total value.

As examples of how to avoid premature salary negotiation, consider the following dialogs:

> *Interviewer: What is your salary range?*
>
> *Candidate: Honestly, I don't have a salary range. There are so many things to take into account such as what the people I would be working with are like, the type of work, the benefits, and so forth that it's not something I could estimate at this point.*
>
> *Interviewer: If we offered you a base salary of $61,000 per year, what is your "gut feeling" Would you take the job?*
>
> *Candidate: I appreciate your honesty and frankness. I hope you will appreciate mine as well—salary is not something I am considering right now. I'm afraid I haven't conducted any research on compensation yet. I will have to get back to you.*
>
> *Interviewer: What will it take money-wise for you to take a job with us?*
>
> *Candidate: I don't have any set numbers—compensation is definitely negotiable.*

Although rare, you may be put in a situation where you absolutely must state some sort of salary expectations to the employer or the hiring process cannot continue. In such a situation it is recommended that you give a focus area, i.e. "well, my main concern is my base salary because I want to ensure that I have enough to support myself and am paid what I am worth for the skills I bring to the table" or "I am less worried about my base salary and more concerned that my relocation is funded entirely, with no ongoing debt to myself. I do not want to start out my career with debt."

If you decide to negotiate and have an offer in-hand, it is critical to gather essential facts. Be certain of your worth for the position. Statistics such as "the average industrial engineering new-hire in California makes 51,000 dollars a year" can be invaluable when negotiating salary. The following sections will cover evaluating the total worth of offers and finding compensation-related information.

What do you actually say when negotiating? A strong approach to negotiation is to focus on the needs of the employer. Emphasize how your accomplishments can help the organization meet its goals. Speaking to your hiring manager directly is usually a more successful strategy, but who you talk to depends on who you are most comfortable with and where the organization directs you. Consider the following approach:

Hiring manager: Hello Brett. I'm glad to hear from you again.

Candidate: It's my pleasure to talk to you again as well Jeff. I've spent a considerable amount of time looking over the offer letter you sent a few days ago and, if you have a moment, I'd like to give you some feedback.

Hiring manager: Of course.

Candidate: I think the description of the position you're offering is directly in line with my expectations for starting a bright career. Also, the people I interviewed with seem like a fantastic team. Kevin and Jackie were great, I hope I have a chance to work with everyone I met.

Hiring manager: I agree. I've certainly never worked with a better group of people.

Candidate: After doing a bit of research, talking with my university career counselor, and consulting some of my friends that work in your industry, I've found that an average entry-level chemical engineer with my degree makes $53,000 a year in Louisiana. So, from what I can tell, your offer matches the state's average salary. I've also observed that it seems as though the numbers don't really add up compared to another offer I have in a different city. The difference is a little over 8 percent in total compensation.

Hiring manager: We have kind of a standard process for putting together offers. I'm afraid we don't have much freedom to change the numbers.

Candidate: I completely understand. I hope you appreciate my honesty—I just want to make sure you know what's on my mind. The truth is, I believe this position to be the best fit for my skill-set and career goals. I think you would agree that I have a strong research background in polymers and my previous work with Dow Chemical puts me in a position to add great value to your team. I feel that I would fit right in and contribute from the beginning.

> **Hiring manager:** *I definitely agree. We think you were by far the best candidate out of the ten we looked at.*
>
> **Candidate:** *Most university hires come out of college and do not really add full productivity value to their employer for months. I think my ability to help your team succeed is at least in the top ten percent in comparison to my peers. As much as I want to work with you, I feel uncomfortable coming on with an average salary for our field when I know I can do a better job than the average chemical engineer.*
>
> *I think it's clear that I can bring value to your organization, but I see a risk that perhaps that value would not be recognized in my career development. So, what I'd like to talk about is how to mitigate that risk. I know your hiring practices are very structured. I'm certainly willing to be flexible; base salary is not the only thing that I consider compensation.*
>
> **Hiring manager:** *You know, if I was in your position I would be asking the same questions. Perhaps our compensation system needs to be updated a bit. To be honest, I haven't looked at the numbers very closely myself. Maybe we can work something out. I'll talk to HR and try to find out what we can do.*

A final point about compensation is that monetary rewards are not the only negotiable term. You can also negotiate:

- *Your job title.* If you have aspirations for writing trade articles or for contributing to professional communities it may be beneficial to negotiate a custom job title. A strong job title can help you to gain visibility within the company or may stand out on your resume for future interviewing.

- *Training.* Employers often provide world-class training such as management courses, conferences, and certifications which are inaccessible or very costly otherwise.

- *Travel.* Some organizations offer rotational programs covering different sites or opportunities for business travel.

- *The type of work and location.* For many candidates, the location or type of work is very important. Unlike other types of compensation, it is recommended that you disclose your preferences for job responsibilities or a site location early in the interview process.

EVALUATING OFFERS

It is crucial to calculate the total value of offers. HR representatives can sometimes glaze over critical details by saying something like "the benefits are standard." This section goes over common components of compensation packages and shows you what you'll need to ask. Consider the following forms of compensation:

- *Cost-of-living.* This is often the most significant consideration outside of the annual salary offered. The cost of living is primarily affected by state taxes, commuting miles to work, and rental or mortgage costs. For example, the difference between New York City and Orlando, Florida is over 60 percent. Very few companies offer a cost-of-living adjustment to match such differences. You may be able to offset some of the costs by finding an exceptional deal on housing, but gas prices, state sales tax, and income tax are unavoidable. The "Compensation related research" section cites sources to find cost-of-living figures.

- *Signing bonuses.* A signing bonus can be directly added to your total monetary compensation. Be sure to ask whether it is a tax-assisted signing bonus. This means you get the full amount after taxes. If it is not tax-assisted, you'll only see about 60% of the stated amount. You may also want to ask whether it is a retention bonus which means you have to repay the organization the bonus if you leave before a certain date.

- *Bonuses.* Annual bonuses can be very difficult to evaluate. The policy for yearly bonuses varies tremendously among different organizations. Try to find out what an average new-hire got the previous year. It is often the case that bonuses only go to a the most "valuable" employees, which means managers get bonuses and new-hires only get them under unusual circumstances. Additionally, an HR representative may give you the cap for what is possible for a bonus which is rarely reached. Find out what defines the bonus percentage—your performance or the organization's performance as a whole.

- *Stock purchasing options.* An employee stock purchase plan allows an employee to buy a certain amount of company stock at a discounted price. For example, an employer may allow you to buy stock at a discount of 15% from the lowest price within the past six months with as much as 30% of your salary. A quick way to evaluate this is to add 1% to the discount percentage for every month in the pricing period and multiplying that percentage by your intended investment in the program. For the figures stated above and an investment of

$10,000 this would be $1,600. Keep in mind that all profits from stocks are taxed by the government because of capital gains tax (the money you invest is never taxed, only the gains or capital).

- *Stock awards.* In the case of a stock award, the company gives you some of their stock for free. Be sure to ask about the vesting policy. Although the stocks are in your name when they are awarded to you, you can only sell the percentage you are vested in. For example, the offer may state that 25% is vested per year. Thus, you would need to stay at the company for 4 years to truly own all of the promised stock. When adding stock awards, only add the amount that will be vested for the period of time you are evaluating after taxes. For example, if you are calculating total compensation for your first two years of work, multiply the amount vested after two years by the current stock price and 70% (for taxes).

- *Tuition reimbursement.* If you are certain that you will seek more education, you can add the cost of tuition to your total compensation if the employer offers tuition reimbursement. Be sure to check if the employer has a yearly cap.

- *401(K) retirement plans.* A 401(K) account is basically an investment account that is not taxed. Since it is government regulated and intended for retirement, you can't take money out until you retire (see http://www.irs.gov/taxtopics/ tc424.html). Not only do you get an automatic 30% increase in cash relative to your investment because of the tax break, but employers often mirror your contributions. For instance, assume your employer matches your contributions up to 6% of your salary which is $3,000. Assuming $3,000 is your annual contribution, your added compensation is $900 from the tax break and $3,000 from the employer's contribution.

- *Health benefits.* This includes medical coverage, dental coverage, and vision coverage. Health benefits coverage has the potential to reduce your total compensation rather than increase it. In general, there are three ways this can happen—through co-payments, monthly payments, and yearly deductibles. For example, let's assume you see a doctor four times a year and a dentist twice a year with each visit costing a total of $100. Assuming your employer requires a co-payment of 30% per visit and a monthly payment of $25, your yearly medical costs are $480. Assuming the monthly payments of $25 are replaced with a yearly deductible of $500, your yearly medical costs are $525.

- *Tax-free health accounts.* Often called flex accounts, these allow you to set aside money for medical costs ranging from band-aids to surgeries before taxes. You can calculate the worth of this benefit by taking the amount you intend to set aside and multiplying it by 30%. Some employers donate to a health savings account on a yearly basis which can be added directly to your total compensation.

- *Relocation.* Employers nearly always provide relocation assistance. Their policy for relocation can both decrease or increase your offer's value. If you are not assisted with travel expenses, shipping, packing, or a temporary house hunting trip, these are expenses which can lower your total compensation. If they offer a relocation bonus, ask whether it is tax-assisted and estimate how much you will use.

Sample Offer Evaluation

To illustrate how to compute the total value of an offer, a brief sample offer letter follows:

Sample offer information

Melissa,

We are pleased to extend you an offer of full-time employment. We are excited about your interest in our organization and look forward to having you.

You are invited to join the cryptography department at a weekly salary of $1,050 dollars. We are also pleased to offer a sign-on award of $4,100 pending your signature of the attached documents. You are also eligible to receive a yearly bonus of 2% to 8% of your annual salary depending on your performance and productivity.

We are proud to offer a competitive retirement savings plan. You can contribute up to 5% of your weekly salary on a before-tax basis to a retirement account which is automatically matched by our contributions. Additional unmatched contributions can be added up to certain IRS limitations (see the attached documents).

You are eligible to receive full medical and dental coverage without monthly payments or visit co-payments (a yearly deductible of $700 does apply). You are also eligible to be part of the Health Savings Account (HSA) program which is a tax-free account that can be used for any medical cost not covered by medical and dental plans. The value of your HSA is not lost at the end of the year since its balance roles over. For details regarding available health benefits please see the attached benefits packet.

To assist you with your transition to Baltimore, a tax-assisted lump sum of $500 will be provided for your expenses. Additionally, a relocation consultant can be assigned to make the transition as convenient as possible.

We look forward to receiving your decision no later than February 21st.

It is rare to get all the information you need in one place as shown in the letter above. The letter is also quite brief compared to a typical offer letter. It is more realistic to acquire all the information from various sources including the offer letter, company benefits websites, and communication with a recruiter or other HR representative.

Now let's break down the information and calculate the total monetary value. Items with a '+' indicate an increase in total compensation and a '-' indicates a decrease. It is critical to calculate an estimate that reflects the dollars you would receive in-hand. This is because many benefits provide tax breaks or penalties which are not factored in if you do a before-tax analysis. For simplicity, a 30% tax rate is assumed.

Another consideration is how to weigh temporary compensation such as signing bonuses. They definitely impact your total compensation, but simply adding temporary compensation to the total doesn't reflect what your compensation will be past the first year. A good compromise is to estimate the total compensation for the first two years of work which is the approach used in the following analysis:

Annual salary (+)

Assuming two weeks of vacation, the weekly salary will be paid fifty times annually. Keep in mind that 30% needs to be deducted for taxes:

2 years x 50 weeks x $1,050 x 70% =**$73,500**

Signing bonus (+)
Assuming the bonus is not tax-assisted:

$4,100 x 70% =**$2,870**

Annual bonus (+)
Assuming annual bonuses of five percent that are not tax-assisted:

$73,500 x 5% =**$3,675**

401(K) plan (+)
Assuming Melissa contributes 7% of her salary with a before-tax 2-year salary of $105,000:

$105,000 x 7% x 30% + $105,000 x 5% =**$7,455**

Health benefits (-)
Assuming Melissa spends at least $700 a year on medical payments:

2 years x $700 =**$1,400**

Tax-free health account (+)
Assuming $800 is contributed to the HSA account annually:

2 years x $800 x %30 =**$480**

Relocation bonus (-)
$500 is rarely enough for relocation. A drive or airline ticket alone may exhaust the lump sum. Assuming relocation will cost $1500:

$1500 - $500 =**$1,000**

Total 2-year projection
$73,500 + $2,870 + $3,675 + $7,455 - $1,400 + $480 - $1,000 =**$85,580**

Of course, the calculated 2-year compensation total is most useful when comparing offers. Also, this calculation did not consider cost-of-living which is usually of significant importance. Finally, be sure to take into account any special financial needs you have. For example, many employers provide financial assistance for daily child care or rollover paid vacation.

COMPENSATION RELATED RESEARCH

Your best reference is your university. Most career resource centers provide statistics on salary by major and have excellent resources for compensation-related research. Your next best reference is likely to be your peers. If your network includes someone who has worked for an organization in the industry you are considering, it can be very beneficial to get their insights on evaluating compensation. Be careful though as individuals tend to exaggerate or add bonuses to base salary. For some online resources, consider the following websites:

General

- *http://content.salary.monster.com/archives/negotiations*—*Monster.com negotiation advice*

- http://www.careerjournal.com/salaryhiring/negotiate—*The Wall Street Journal Executive Career Site*

Cost-of-living

- http://www.bestplaces.net—*Sperling's Best Places*

- http://www.salary.com—*Salary.com*

Salary Related

- http://www.jobstar.org/tools/salary/sal-prof.cfm—*Job Star Central*

- www.salaryexpert.com—*Salary Expert.com*

CREATING ALLIES OUT OF HUMAN RESOURCE REPRESENTATIVES

HR representatives are often very informed about the inner workings of an organization. Since they are motivated to provide you with information about the company, use this to your advantage! In some cases an HR representative may be coordinating many events and candidates so you may want to test the waters by sending a question by email first. If an HR representative calls you fairly often and is anxious to accommodate your needs, this is a sure sign that they are open to questions. What should you ask? Just about anything from *Chapter4: Researching an Organization*. Also, consider the following:

Before Interviews

- *How the company is organized.* You may want to ask an HR representative the organizational structure of the group that is interviewing. This information can prove to be very impressive during interviews.

- *The management chain for the position.* Similar to the organizational structure, find out who the leading management is for the group hiring.

- *What the culture is like.* This can help you fit-in especially for social type interviewing such as lunch interviews.

- *Information on their products.* You may be able to gain valuable insight to match your past experiences to their needs. They are not likely to be subject matter experts, but probably can point you to the best resources. Be sure you have a high-level understanding of the products before approaching any representative of an organization.

After an offer

- *Promotional opportunities.* You may want to find out what to expect for a career progression. An approach you can take is to ask for an example of a recent new-hire that has done well.

- *Salary progression.* Determine the pay grade (or level, band, range, etc.) you are being offered and how the system works.

- *Performance reviews.* You can ask how your performance will be reviewed. Many organizations have formal processes where employees write goals to management and are held accountable to those goals at the end of the year.

- *Cost-of-living related information.* You can ask for references to apartment or housing agencies to get an estimate of living expenses.

- *Save your relationship with HR representatives.* If you build a good relationship with someone in the company's HR organization, they can lookout for you throughout your career. Even if you decide to work elsewhere, you never know when you'll be looking for a job. The more people you know, the more doors it will open.

HOW TO DECLINE AN OFFER

If you decide to decline an employer's offer, it is important to take some time and formulate your thoughts. How you handle the situation can reflect on your university, degree program, and your future employer. It is important to keep a good relationship with everyone you meet because they may become valuable additions to your network. The organization extending the offer is likely to remember you if you handle the entire interviewing process gracefully. The relationships you keep should prove useful if you ever need an industry insider or a contact for future positions. Here are some other considerations:

- *Do not dwell on negative reasons for declining an offer.* Unless the organization specifically asks, avoid listing reasons for your decision. Remember, your goal is to keep relationships.

- *Avoid focusing on the other organization.* You may be tempted to rant on about how wonderful the other company is and how you are excited about it. Your message should be about them, not about you or the other company.

- *Stay positive.* Try to think about the positive things that happened throughout the interview process. If you met fascinating people or the process impressed you in some way, be sure to mention it.

If you are comfortable and are a strong communicator over the phone, it is best give the people you met a call. Otherwise, here is a sample email that was actually used by one of the contributors to this book:

Subject: Offer decision

After careful consideration and after consulting mentors, family, and trusted friends—I have accepted an employment offer from a different organization. It is my belief that Microsoft is an outstanding company; I'm honored that I was offered an opportunity to be a part of your team.

I want to personally thank Ted, Lora, Amy, and everyone else who I had the pleasure of meeting for their time and gracious company.

Sincerely,

Full Name

COMMON MISTAKES

1. *Negotiating salary before receiving an offer.* The most important rule of compensation negotiation is to wait until you have an offer in-hand.

2. *Stating that you only want to stay at the company for a few years.* This is basically stating that you cannot be retained and are likely to create a high turnover cost.

3. *Hinting that you want to get an MBA or Ph.D. as soon as possible.* Unless you intend to do this part-time at a local university, you are stating that you intend to leave in the near future.

4. *Not factoring in cost-of-living.* At least find out if there is a difference in state taxes.

5. *Declining an offer unprofessionally.* There is no reason to burn a bridge unnecessarily.

Profile
Carl Irvine

Who do you work for, what is your official job title, and where is the job located?

I'm a Process Engineer II for Georgia-Pacific at their paper mill in Palatka, FL.

Was it your first choice?

Yes. I was also considering the semiconductor industry, oil industry, or working for the federal government. I chose GP in order to work for a company that makes a product that is an end-user consumer product. During my co-op for Intersil, a semiconductor company, I felt I was working on a small component you don't really come in contact with in everyday life—I felt like a middleman. I also wanted to be a part of a very stable industry. I realized that the semiconductor industry is cyclical which means periodic layoffs.

What are some positive aspects of the job?

I work in a diverse, interdisciplinary environment covering every aspect of engineering. The workforce at the mill spans the operators with a high school education all the way to Ph.D. level professionals such as the Technical Superintendant.

I'm constantly learning and being challenged. Innovation matters—it is key in finding new ways to improve efficiency and reduce costs. I also like the structured entry-level engineering program they offer which paired me with an experienced mentor rather than just throwing me to the wolves.

What are some negative aspects?

The hours to perform my job effectively exceeded my expectations.

What is your typical day like?

I start work at around 6:30 AM. There is a 30-minute maintenance meeting where we review the maintenance work for the day, planning for the week, and discuss where to focus the man power available. Then we have a 30-minute production meeting discussing issues regarding quality, cost, and efficiency for the mill's process flow.

The next five hours can involve a number of things including planning, communication with peers and outside resources such as vendors, calculating costs for the accounting group, and working with production operators to fix process problems. Sometimes I participate in a mill improvement program called "Vision" which gets a team together to focus on a single problem or goal.

Then, I'm off to lunch for about 30-minutes. I try to eat lunch with different people everyday. For example, co-workers, technical analysts (who work in chemical labs collecting data), operators in different control rooms, etc. The relationships I have made during lunch are invaluable. A lot of the operators and technicians really respond when I need something done or have a question because I know them at a personal level. Most of the problems in the process are found by the operators so I rely on them a lot.

I then try to get three hours of productive work done consisting of the same activities I engage in before lunch. I try to get eight hours of real productivity in for a ten hour day. After lunch, I often get signatures for chemical trials, look at chemical research, and get recommendations for what I should work on next.

At 2 PM we have another maintenance meeting. This is critical to keeping the mill running as we discuss what overtime work needs to be done and what resources are needed by 6 AM the next morning. I usually leave work at 5 PM.

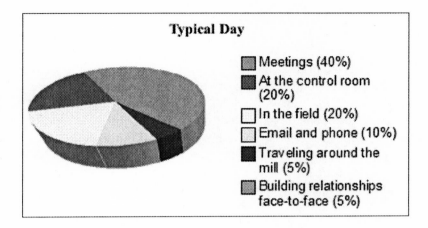

How did you make initial contact with Georgia-Pacific?

I knew they were going to recruit at my university in an upcoming career fair. I researched the company extensively—I spent about four hours reading online.

I went to an information sessions for Georgia-Pacific the night before my university career fair. I was able to spend one-on-one time with the human resource manager. I also met the mill manager and several engineers. The next day at the career fair, they remembered me—I wasn't just another face.

After the career fair, I received an email invitation for an on-campus interview.

What was your campus interview like?

It was mainly a behavioral interview focused on prior experience. I was asked whether I liked a "clean" environment. I realized that they were not interviewing for an office style engineering position so I talked to them about how I like to work on my car. We also spent a lot of time talking about the Palatka area, the family life there, and expectations of the position.

What was your site interview like?

It was a large event in Baton Rouge, Louisiana which lasted 3-days and 2-nights. We had various group sessions in teams of five. For example, we had a competition where we were given a box of materials. There were no rules other than "build the biggest, longest bridge you can." It was a very interesting test of character, creativity, innovation, leadership, follower ship, and humility. By the way, my team came in second.

The last day consisted of three interviews. The first few had two interviewers per-candidate and the last one had four interviewers per candidate. I was asked to rank my preferences for different locations and professions. The choices for engineering professions were process engineering, process control, capital project engineering, power generation, chemical recovery, and paper machinery.

I noticed that they asked a lot about my personal interests. I think they wanted to make sure I was cut out for a 24/7, hands-on production environment.

Have any memorable questions?

They asked for a specific example of when I had failed. I gave an example during my time as an intern for Intersil. At the time, I was working with the production of the actual product, on the silicon wafers, and I over-developed the wafers. After realizing my mistake, I immediately told my superiors that I had done something wrong. We found an innovative way to salvage all six wafers saving the company roughly 15,000 chips.

I was also asked how I would handle the situation of instructing someone to perform a task in a production environment. The first observation I made about the question was that a production environment is dynamic and loud; most likely, requiring ear plugs! I recommended starting in a quite room with documentation, diagrams, and verbal instruction. I then suggested having the trainee do a trial run at the task in the field. Finally, after observing the trainee's performance, I recommended more time in a quite area to discuss any further feedback.

What advice do you have for dealing with human resource representatives?

Learn their names and get them right.

They are looking for people that are stable so don't hold back on giving them information on any factor which indicates stability in your life such as future goals, mentioning that you are married, etc. The HR representatives at Georgia-Pacific seem to like people that get involved in the community. I think they see a strong correlation between strong contributors to the company and generous contributors to the community.

Make their job easy—managing the administrative details of dozens of candidates can be unforgiving. Make sure they always have your contact information as well.

Human resource representatives that do paperwork can also answer a lot of key questions. For example, they may have insights on what the current "pain" for company management is at the time or know what managers are the best to work under. Always be curious about what they do and what their role is. Ask what they did before their HR job. They may have started somewhere else—maybe even in the same position you are considering.

CARL IRVINE

cirvine03@aol.com
2447 Golf View Dr
Orange Park, FL 32003
(904) 215-3934

OBJECTIVE

Obtain a challenging full-time chemical engineering position where I can apply classroom knowledge and internship experiences.

RELATED EXPERIENCE

1/2003-5/2003   **Intersil Corporation: Process Engineering Intern**
Developed a 21-page Canon Stepper Matching Manual for the photo engineering team
Presented research findings to management and engineering on process changes for Canon Stepper matching procedures and measurement marks for metrology tools
Optimized measurement files on metrology tools for pattern recognition of photo resist
Worked with the photo engineering team to achieve a reduced rework rate
Commited to a 50-60 hour engineering work week
Acquired skills needed to effectively communicate in a high stress enviroment

5/2002-8/2002   **Intersil Corporation: Process Engineering Intern**
Presented research findings to management and engineering in order to implement Shipley SPR850 Photo Resist for production on submicron technologies
Worked on a team with process engineers who installed, qualified and optimized tool sets to increase production capacity in a silicon wafer fabrication facility
Gained proficiency in operating and calibrating the following tool sets: SVG 90 Coaters, SVG 90 Developers and Metra 2100 (a metrology tool)
Gained proficiency in creating job-decks for the following tool sets: Hitachi SEM and Canon Steppers (Models I3, I5 and IW)

2/1999-Present   **University of Florida Computing Help Desk: Senior Consultant Supervisor**
Supervised, trained and provided leadership for a staff of 8-12 computer consultants
Coordinated technical solutions between first- and second-level technical support groups
Interviewed, hired and trained new computer technical consultants
Gained problem-solving skills to diagnose computer problems

EDUCATION

University of Florida
Bachelor of Science in Chemical Engineering (Expected graduation: 12/2003)
GPA: 3.1 on a 4.00 scale
Bachelor of Arts in Sociology (Graduated: 12/2001)

ASSOCIATED SKILLS

Computer Languages: HTML, C Programming, Visual Basic
Operating Systems: Windows 95, 98, NT4, ME, 2000, XP, UNIX and Macintosh OS
Application Software: Microsoft Office, Outlook, Adobe Photoshop and HYSYS Computer Modeling
Internet Applications: Netscape, SSH, Telnet, FTP and numerous E-mail clients

HONORS/AFFILIATIONS/ACTIVITIES

UF Dean's List: Fall and Spring 2001, Spring 2002 and Summer 2003
ChemE Car Design Competition: 1st Place-2001 Southern Regional Conference, 6th Place-2001 National Conference
AIChE Executive Council Secretary (2001) and Student Affiliate
Student Affiliate of the American Chemical Society
Habitat for Humanity Volunteer
VA Medical Center Volunteer
Advanced SCUBA and Lifegaurd Certified

978-0-595-36681-1
0-595-36681-3

Printed in the United States
43119LVS00004B/112